INTO

THE TANGLE OF

FRIENDSHIP

BOOKS BY BETH KEPHART

A Slant of Sun: One Child's Courage

Into the Tangle of Friendship

Into
the Tangle
of Friendship:

A MEMOIR OF THE
THINGS THAT
MATTER

BETH KEPHART

In friendship,

Beth Kephart

HOUGHTON MIFFLIN COMPANY · BOSTON · NEW YORK

2000

For information about permission to reproduce selections
from this book, write to Permissions, Houghton Mifflin Company,
215 Park Avenue South, New York, New York 10003.

Visit our Web site: www.houghtonmifflinbooks.com

Library of Congress Cataloging-in-Publication Data
Kephart, Beth.
    Into the tangle of friendship : a memoir of
    the things that matter / Beth Kephart.
        p.   cm.
    ISBN 0-618-03387-4
    1. Kephart, Beth.   2. Friendship.   I. Title.
CT275.K45855 A3 2000
158.2'5—dc21   00-038915

Book design by Anne Chalmers
Typefaces: Janson Text, Type Embellishments, Futura T

Printed in the United States of America

QUM 10 9 8 7 6 5 4 3 2 1

Parts of Chapter 11, "Being There," appeared in very different form
in *The Leap Years: Women Reflect on Change, Loss, and Love*, edited by
Mary Anne Maier and Joan Shaddox Isom (Beacon Press, 1999).
Parts of Chapter 14, "From Silence Grows," appeared in very different form in *Iowa Woman* (August 1992).

FOR BILL,
for then, for now, for always,

AND FOR JEREMY,
whose wisdom startles and appeases

Contents

Prologue

CALL THE WOODEN CLIMBER in the center the seat of power. Call the sandbox and the swings and the splintered tables the hearts of commerce; the shade beneath the oaks, the church; the ravaged muddy creek beyond, this country's borderlands. It is spring—a puckering day. The kids—alone, in pairs, afraid, delighted, in cars, on foot, in a parade of rusty wagons, on the verge of brave entanglements—have finally come.

Out on the playground's edge, the sun at my back, I sit and wait and wonder. I watch. I know that the coming hours will shape the children's view of friendship and, consequently, their view of themselves. I know that there will be struggles, winners, losers, so many one-act plays, mysteries and parables. Who is the leader here, and who the disciple? Who will betray, who can be trusted? Who will be drawn in, who locked out? How will passions coalesce, what will be talked about, who will care? When will the accretion of events, hopes, revelations, gifts, become the stuff of memory and faith, a durable philosophy of friendship?

The playground bristles. The kids keep coming. A red-cheeked boy with banged-up knees ascends the climber and declares himself king. Below him, in the pit of oyster-colored sand, an artist marvels at his own crystalline creation, then guards its sanctity from the others. Blond and uncompromising, plastic molds and shovels at his feet, he attracts a gaggle of little girls and boys, beguiles them with the magic of the sand. One or two watch in reverent awe: obedient, an audience. The others grow rowdy, impatient, seize the artist's tools, plot a sandbox revolution. A tussle over ownership and rules ensues until some kids run off and some decide to stay, and the morning readjusts to new rhythms and old patterns. Soon boys are dissecting bugs beneath a tree, kids are fishing for algae in the creek, girls are scraping bare toes against the sun as mothers, fathers, nannies, siblings push them higher on the swings.

Amid all of this, one child stands forlorn on the fringe—a boy without a place to play in this prolific spring. His bucket dangling over his wrist like a bracelet, his hair rolled up like SpaghettiOs beneath a cap, he has come too late, or too timid, and he has come alone. Sitting where I am, the sun now warmer at my back, I imagine how his mind is working, how his heart is feeling, how heavy his bucket feels across his wrist. I imagine that I know him, and in some ways, I'm sure I do. For I too have come alone. I—mother, wife, daughter, sister, friend—wait here, on the brink.

Watching the boy in the baseball cap, watching the others in their silliness and seriousness, their clear unrivaled laughter, I am taken back to years ago when I chose my friends, then they chose me. Friendship, from the very start, was both exotic and pragmatic, a roughing up and a letting down. It was the way I shared what I loved and discovered what was worth sharing; the way I wasted the day, or fractions of day; the way I knew how big or strong or good or protected or likable I—for that small instant—was. Friendship happened in neighborhoods and classrooms, and lasted for seconds and years. It turned trees into castles and marbles into coins, the streamers on a tricycle into wings of plastic glory.

This story, I know, is everybody's story, for the capacity and desire for friendship are scripted right into our genes. Rousseau's lonely heroes notwithstanding, we are intrinsically social creatures, our very survival inextricably linked to the fabrics we weave ourselves into. Six billion people now throb upon our planet; six billion people must somehow daily get along—organize resources, divvy up jewels, agree to certain customs, share the wonder of a baby's face or an aurora borealis. Sometimes the entanglements leave us with bruises, sometimes with friendships, and at times, of course, friendships leave us hurting, and we start all over again. Friendship isn't merely the province of photo albums and light romance; it should not, as it so often is, be taken for granted, a random given. Sociability—and, by extension, friendship—is, as poet and social philosopher Terrence Des Pres once noted, the by-product of the self-preserving forces of evolution.

Look at the boy in his crumpled baseball cap. Look at how he stands: a muted wanting, his bucket empty.

Throughout our lives, friends enclose us, like pairs of parentheses. They shift our boundaries, crater our terrain. They fume through the cracks of our tentative houses, and parts of them always remain. They are the antidote not to our aloneness, but to our loneliness. I think of someone sliding over on a bench. A chair being added to a circle. A letter sent for no good reason. A joke only two people understand. I think of the way an oak's roots hunger after water, suck life into the tree, anchor the pith, the heartwood, the windshake, the phloem, and keep the branches in their leaves. I think of someone looking up and saying, *Hey, I'm glad to see you.* Someone indulging in the mathematics of plurals and finding more than expected in the sum. Friendship asks and wants, hollows and fills, ages with us and we through it, cradles us, finally, like family. It is ecology and mystery and language, all three. Fantastic, sustaining, bewildering, it requires us to explore and respect its multiplicity of forms and to teach our children its many lessons. To visit playgrounds where it all begins and wait and watch and remember.

I want to know what friendship is because I am a woman, nearly forty. I want to know because I am a wife, fifteen years married. I want to know because an old best friend has found her way back to my life, like a leaf on the wind, like a cure, and because some friends have gone missing, and others are in pain, and others give me gifts so large I cannot reciprocate. I want to know what friendship is because I am the mother of a boy of grace and humor, a storyteller, a listener, a kid who is happily, confidently off on his own at school, messing around with his own band of friends, knocking soccer goals home at recess, settling down to a geography test and getting everything, save one trick spelling, correct. I am the mother of a boy named Jeremy who is deep in his own becoming, standing on the precipice of time. What do I teach him about friendship? What do I know? What can I remember and elucidate and put upon this page that will help him build a life through friendship, stretch his living across its poles?

What do any of us know about friendship, isn't that the question here? What can we make of how it changes over time, how it is about wonder at first, then self-definition, then survival, how it is always about comfort, about simply being here, alive? How do we come to terms with the responsibilities and limitations, the possibility of schisms and despair? Because isn't it true that the more we let others into our lives, the safer we become and also the more endangered. Isn't it worth it nonetheless? Friendships matter; they rebut death, they tie us to this earth, and, when we're gone, they keep us here; our friends remember us. Looking back and looking forward we see that this is true: friendship stands as both a scaffolding and a bridge.

The boy with the baseball cap is standing before me. He is a lonely alone, his curls spiraling out in all directions. The artist and his fans have settled in. The king now has a queen and two loud princes. The boys beneath the tree have given up on their disassembled bug. The bouncy horses bounce and bounce, the swings draw arcs through the air, and down the slope by the creek, algae hangs like a bright flag on a stick.

"Hey," I say to the boy with the cap. "Hey. How about we build us a village?"

"Yeah?" he says, startled. He had not noticed me before.

"Yeah," I offer. "A village. Right here. In our private corner of the sand."

"Sure, yeah," he says. "Whatever," his voice wincing and grateful. Dropping to his knees, a shy, heavy gesture, he scoops his hands into the sand and starts prodding, poking, plunging. Beside him, I too drop to my knees and steep my hands, pull the sand up into my cupped fingers and let it sift through; pull it up again, watch the grains fleck with light and filter, fall. I am remembering, making sense of things, remembering. My hands pull the sand up, let it go, plow deeper and deeper into the earth. Friendship is a benefaction and a weight. It is an instruction and a tool, a risk, a therapeutic, a happenstance, a philosophy. I must find the words to teach my son. Digging for water, digging for roots, I listen to the soft susurrus of earth hitting earth, then hear a burst of laughter nearby. It's the boy beside me, elbow-deep in the sand. The kid with the cap and a bucket full of sand, who is, for now, not lonely.

INTO

THE TANGLE OF

FRIENDSHIP

I

Looping
Back In

THIS IS THE MEMORY of a blonde girl on the sidewalk of a new street. The girl wears white, and she sizzles. I am nearby, timid, holding my mother's hand, but now I let it go in favor of this most alluring blonde. Arms outstretched, I skip behind her as she quivers up a path that leads to a door, then passes through the door and down a hallway that leads to a long, wide, windowed room. Swans, that's it. She is the white swan, and what else would I be but the black? And this is where it begins—a dance, a flickering of light and shadow across the room. I following. She teaching. I inveigled into utter transformation, so that when I touch my hair, it's feathers. Do we own the house? Are we alone? Did someone put the music on, or has it always been playing?

Remember her name now. Remember Denise. And what did she grow up to be, who is she now, this true forever friend?

Denise down the street was my very first best friend. Together we were silly, we were naughty, we got into deepest, darkest trouble for peeing side by side in two navy blue buckets. Denise grew up prettier and prettier, but my family moved away and then moved back, and then my father was relocated again. We were uprooted, we moved back, and by the time I was nine, I couldn't make room for being pretty. I was the girl by the creek with her pant legs rolled up, and Denise was in tutus and lace. At the bend in the street squatted a low, dark rancher, where the new girl, Kelly, lived. She had gravitated to the creek as I had, and she showed me what was marvelous about holding tadpoles in one hand.

I have in my possession only two photographs of me at nine years old. In one I'm licking milk-chocolate batter from a smothered kitchen whip; in the other I'm standing with Kelly. It is 1969, and her charcoal tee is emblazoned with an American flag; it's June, warm, the last day of school, and she's wearing jeans and a biker jacket. Her glasses alone keep her thick hair out of her eyes. She holds a lime-colored pencil like a baton. Her dad is in the house and the TV is on. I don't remember her mother.

I stand beside Kelly wearing a Butterick—a white cotton affair with a waffle texture, trimmed along the hem and sleeves with a diaphanous rose-patterned fabric. Three smooth decorative buttons perch near the collar. When I look at this hand-sewn dress in the fading photograph I consider how hard my mother worked on behalf of her three kids.

I don't wear the Butterick well. I wear—and I remember the argument—knee socks instead of tights, sneakers instead of shoes. My hair is a dark brown aura of misbehaving curls, and there's a sweetness about me, as well as a bite. Looking at that photo, I remember the lessons of that odd, unlikely friendship, remember how I came to know that friendship has a price. I knew where I had to sit on the bus, understood who I got to play with at recess, came to terms with the fact that when the nice, easy family up the street conducted its annual back-yard circus, I would be invited to pay for tickets but would not, as so many other neighborhood kids were, be invited to perform. Endless repercussions spring from palling around with or buddying up or whispering some secret to another. There is no simplicity in choosing the hippie girl from the darkest house as one's dearest, bestest friend. Friendship is deflective, defining, dividing; it both expands and delimits. It is a vulnerability of a most peculiar kind, a melding into, a vessel: made. When I look back I see my friends, I see myself, and I wonder just who fashioned whom. Either way, one makes the other. Either way, something swells and something cleaves off, broken.

In the theater of family hang the scintillas of friends. I learned young that all families are porous, osmotic, forever redefined and shifted by the friends we bring home, the stories they tell, the residues and mysteries they leave behind. Kelly was my friend, but she was also, indisputably, part of my family—part of the questions my mother, father, brother, sister asked, part of the plans we made, part of our compromising, our negotiating, our blood work, part of our dinner table, our laughter, our encouragement, our praise. Denise, too, was a link in the family chain: we all knew and embraced her, we all were changed by having known her; she was fixed in family memory and lore long after the friendship was over.

My mother's friends were so woven into the rest of us that we gave them family names: Aunt Carol, Aunt Loretta, Aunt Joan. Our house was their house, and their homes were ours, and I was eager, always, to see them, to impart my latest adventure, to find out about theirs. My family would leave town for a while and then come trundling back, and my mother's friends were always there, a circle of safety, a beguiling continuance. I knew their birthdays and sighs, I knew their laughter, their favorite candies, I knew enough about them to imagine both halves of the phone talk I'd hear my mother having when I'd slip, like a secret, into the stairwell at night. At nine, I believed my life would replicate my mother's, that I would collect, like living prayers and trophies, these steadfast familial souls whom my children would call *Aunt* and whose homes would be mine and whom I could love with unwavering abandon.

But for me, at least, such a feat would not come easily. For me, the desire for endless friendship far outweighed my apparent talent for it.

Among the soft pulp of photographs and artifacts in my attic lies no record of the girl who would become my most important teenage friend, save for some final, departing words scrawled in a yearbook on the last day of high school: *I swear to God, I'm still gonna laugh when you're married and pregnant. I swear to God.*

I never heard from her for more than twenty riddled years.

We met when I was thirteen, when I was once again the new girl in another new school, my family having moved again. I got the hang of the cafeteria line. I signed up for one or two teams. I started showing poems to the lit mag committee. I told myself that I had to find friends, that I wouldn't survive in this high school without them. I needed first their protection and their buffer, then their companionship and concern. Then their trust and mine reciprocated, each thing to be acquired in this most elemental order.

There are some people for whom friend making is effortless. They smile, they crack a joke, they shrug insouciantly, they offer something up, accept what has been offered, balance themselves delicately upon the threshold. And when the door unlatches, they're in.

More often than not, though, the launch of a friendship is an imperiled endeavor, requiring the ability to acutely size up the instant at hand and adapt with intelligence, grace, speed. Banter with a stranger is fine, a pleasantry, but what happens when it becomes more than that? When the conversation turns and something chemical sparks and you startle to the possibility that this former stranger who stands beside you at your new high school locker may (and it's only a may) merit more of your time, evolve into a companion or a friend? How do you hold her in *your* sway? Consciously or subconsciously, assessments are made —what you ask next, what you reveal next, how you catch her eye, how you get her to linger, how you form the word *goodbye*. No amount of practice makes the process perfect, for every stranger brings his or her own tempo and neediness to the arrangement. There's plenty of opportunity to err on the side of stinginess or excess, as Willa Cather's novel *My Ántonia* gently reminds us.

"While we snuggled down there out of the wind, she learned a score of words," the novel's narrator, Jim Burden, remembered of his first encounter with the fourteen-year-old Bohemian girl who spoke no English.

She was quick, and very eager. We were so deep on the grass that we could see nothing but the blue sky over us and the gold tree in front of us. It was wonderfully pleasant. After Ántonia had said the new words over and over, she wanted to give me a little chased silver ring she wore on her middle finger. When she coaxed and insisted, I repulsed her quite sternly. I didn't want her ring, and I felt there was something reckless and extravagant about her wishing to give it away to a boy she had never seen before.

So that gifts are fraught and weighted too, parity—some basic equivalency between the thing offered and the thing wanted or deserved—being both elusive and essential to friendship.

In my new high school, I understood that I would have to plan for friendship. I had to think: Who might have room for me? Who isn't taken? I had to shield myself from the hazards of rejection, send out just enough signals but not too many—there's no point, at that age, in broadcasting a need. Walking up and down the halls, I studied students at their lockers, tried on attitudes, sat front, back, middle on the bus. I strategized, adapted, hoped (without disclosing hope) that someone out there was looking, too, that something about me would inspire. One can go one's whole life without a friend; I realized that. There was the possibility of perpetual loneliness, and one had to fight back, defend, or, conversely, take solace from one's solitude.

Into all of this came Joanne, the girl with the soft fringe of lacy hair. She was taller than I, and thin—her long legs perpetually vined around the metal stumps of the classroom chairs. She had the habit of sitting near the front of the class, then glancing behind, repeatedly lifting and shifting the wavy bolt of her hair to get the best view. She had impatient, squirming lips, as if she'd just gotten the hidden joke of the lesson or detected something incongruous.

I admired her brave, beautiful Jewishness. I noticed that she, too, had a brilliant older sibling and a pretty younger sister, that she was nice to me in that awful cafeteria; at her table I always had a place. I noticed how much I wanted to tell her, how I would save stories or make them up for the sake of her reaction. Maybe she came to my house first; that must have been how it was. But after that, I was invited home with her, and we were each other's best friend for four years. Because of Joanne, I learned the music of that era. Because of Joanne, I learned menorahs, dreidels, Israel; I learned to trust my own body and whatever changes it went through; I learned the fine art of passing notes in school.

At school, everyone soon recognized us as a unit. We were stronger, wittier, more attractive combined. We had some kind of allure, some kind of power. Four years went by: birthdays, projects, sleepovers, tedium. We talked on the phone or visited most days of every week, got to know and relax inside each other's families, stood side by side at other classmates' Sweet Sixteens, knew each other's locker combinations. When I spoke of Joanne, she was the noun and the verb. She was the event, the feeling, the actress, the audience. I told Joanne every one of my secrets. Told her what I was afraid of, what I wanted. Senior year, I told Joanne that I had fallen in love.

Of course it was nothing. It was a guy so preposterously and outrageously different from me that I was safe with this crush; it couldn't be reciprocated. I was a runner by then — cross country in winter, track in spring — and he was a middle-distance hero, a back-of-the-bus kind of guy, blond hair hanging over blue eyes, his walk an unattainable swagger. I was head over heels. I loved everything about him. I revealed this, in great detail, to Joanne.

Nightly, every day after school, after homework, after meals, I was upstairs on the phone, combing through details. Whatever he had worn or said, however fast he had run, if he had actually grumbled out some brief hello, I told Joanne. I knew where he lived, I studied his house, I told Joanne. I found out his schedule, the blow by blow; she got the facts. *Maybe he likes you. Really?* I wanted to believe. But he hardly noticed me, and that's the truth, and that's what I know, looking back on it now.

Looking at it then, I was in love. I was hopeful, prayerful, I believed that someday I'd be noticed. Thought I was getting there. Thought, anyway, that he'd soon stop grumbling his hellos. Until Joanne showed up with him at the prom.

When you take a stand on a friendship, when, in rage, you make it clear—*This friendship is over, get out*—you are defining the rest of your life. I didn't know then what I was doing. I didn't know how big the empty space would feel, what successive years would take me through, how my need for friendship and my understanding of it would shift and reshape over time, yet remain a need. I didn't realize then that you can't make old friends, that you can only lose them, that in losing them, you lose part of yourself, a part of your history, the very means, the opportunity to *express* who you are and how you're feeling. You walk around with a void inside that you can never adequately explain.

I went on to college roommates who were nothing like me. After college I shared a tall-ceilinged flat with a woman—she eating dinners in our kitchen with her friends, I reading intently, morosely, indignantly, inside my drafty, lonely room. There was never really another Joanne, another every-single-day best friend, and she didn't see me marry, she didn't know me pregnant. I heard rumors about her, but she was gone. What do you forfeit when you give up a best friendship? Who do you tell your secrets to? I always looked for her, on the street, in the markets, near my birthday.

There is a man on my street who saws off limbs to save his trees. He's eighty, and you can find him in the leaves. If you stop by the curb and call to him in a friendly way, he'll tell you the stories of his birches, his oaks. "This one comes direct from my mother," he once told me, about a tulip tree that's now at least three stories tall. "Came here from her garden at four foot tall; I dug the earth out myself, I laid in the peat moss, I mulched." "Wow," I said. "That's impressive, and it sure is gorgeous." His voice still good for boasting, he replied: "Young lady, here's my secret: it's all about caring. About shaving off the bad parts so that you can save the whole. You love something good enough, you don't let it die." Then he disappeared back into the leaves.

I used to think, when I walked by this man, that he would never have let go of Joanne. He would have shaken off the bad thing. He would have gone toward forgiving. He would have understood that shafting the whole leaves you with nothing but nothing.

The dictionary will gratify nearly any notion of friendship that is floated: either it involves intimacy or it doesn't, requires proof or doesn't, has something or absolutely nothing to do with geography and physical place. Fluid, flexible, transient, unstable, supremely relative—*friendship*, the noun, is a juggler's term, perpetually changing hands. Yet having a friend or not having one, making a friend and being one transcend the imprecisions, become tangible, touchable fact. *She is my friend, and I am hers.*

You are part of his story; he is integral to yours. I took a walk, and I was happy to see them. I've been invited for dinner. These are couplings of words that have roots.

So many possibilities. So many passersby, so much sidewalk talk, so much providence, too many fellow travelers in a crowded train—all of it potentially the beginning of things, all of it potentially nothing. What is the algorithm, the formula whose divine intervention determines friendship anyhow? Of all the conversations we've begun, how many will continue? Of all the faces encountered, what is recalled? *I'll call. I will. I'll write*— but will we really? Lives escape us. Stories do. Acts of friendship go unreturned. Our failure to forgive, to make time, to engage, becomes a terrible haunting.

Once, at a conference I went to, there was a poet, a woman with a euphonious name. Dark eyebrows, light hair, her shirts stopping just above her navel. Lord, she could write. She could describe a wedding dress or the thinness of her mother or the fields camped out east of heart, but it was how she described the things that don't exist that choked me most with surprise. The skies that would not come, the words that swallowed words, the ecstatic snarl of love. Smoke through her lips, dabs of garnet at her neck, a gleam of hair, falling loose—she had, it seemed to me, more words than the rest of us. She had something that everyone who met her simply wanted: *she will be my friend.*

For ten days I imagined a friendship with this poet, a correspondence—writer to writer—that would survive beyond the conference. Increasingly, we found ourselves walking the same lush, vertiginous hill, or making our way to the spot just past the bridge at the swimming hole, where a raft was loose and the children of the authors swam. We would sit in the same slip of the lecture hall or on the same flight of cranky wooden stairs, and she would speak of a house she might paint blue, and I would nod, careful, careful, checking over my shoulder, for always others would come and join in, divert whatever we had been speaking about. I'd drift back and out while the circle around her tightened. You want to be more than you actually are, and you want someone to notice.

Friendship cannot be noosed in or demanded. It cannot, in the end, be contained. We all know that. We learn it at three, four, five—we have to learn it repeatedly through our lifetimes. But what choice did I have, with the poetess headed home? What could I say to this woman, soon escaping? The last night of that conference, I stayed up late and wrote it down. I asked for a chance to stay in touch. *I want to know if your house ever does get painted blue. I want to know about your kettling of words.* If she had tried to write to me what I tried so hard to write to her, there'd have been a swimming of commas, a quick confusion that would have broken apart like light. But she didn't try. Our friendship didn't concern her. There was a postcard once; I have it in the attic. She said she'd drunk the sky.

Friendship is not merely an act of imagination, a desire. It is a pair of eyes turned back, with genuine interest, upon you.

Early last summer, I received a mysterious call—a Joanne, someone was saying, seeking me out. I couldn't and I wouldn't believe it was her; I assumed the message was a prank. Joanne Lang, it said. *Lang.* I thought, *I never knew a Lang.* And if it is Joanne and she really means it, perhaps she'll try again.

And then one early September morning, the phone rang once, and it was Joanne. I knew it before she said anything. I knew the sound of her sigh. The length of the pause between my hello and hers. The shiveriness of her nerves. "Beth?" she asked, after the initial silence. "It's me. Joanne. I've looked for you." I closed my eyes and tried to put myself where she was — another state, an unfamiliar home, a wedding band, perhaps, on her finger. All I could imagine, however hard I tried to see, was that brown lacy hair, draping softly past her shoulder, the twining of her leg around the metal chair, James Taylor on her portable record player, her eyes round and moist as buds. And I remembered how she looked at the prom, and how I must have looked to her, in all my anger.

Not so long ago, Joanne and I had our reunion. At thirty-eight, she looks eighteen; in some ways she is just the way I left her. And yet there are so many unfathomable complications. She's more tender now, more introspective, more relentless with her own intelligence. She's been changed, of course, by the calamities she's lived through, by the friends she's acquired, the family she's made. She's been changed by the passions that have entered her life, and by those that have departed. I learn who she has become through her own modest recollection, a scattering of details. Who are your children? When were they born? What did you look like, Joanne, when you were pregnant? And what became of your mother, and how did you choose the man you married, and what happened to the blond runner, anyway? We move on and away, and other people's lives continue, and sometimes grace will loop us back, but who they've been, minute to minute, change through change, need by need, is gone.

Two years ago, Joanne lost her mother-in-law to cancer; this is the piece of my old best friend that I now, in this moment, best understand. This is the piece she has resurrected most completely, the details she's given me so that I can see. "She gave me my first Christmas, Beth," the lovely Jewess says. "I stood at the top of the steps, staring down at the tree, and I felt giddy as a kid."

Yes, Joanne, I imagine that, I do not say, because my eyes are closed, imagining.

"And when she was dying, when she knew it was the end, I asked her for some sign — something to look for when she was gone. *Ladybugs,* she said. *Every ladybug is me, every ladybug is proof that I am still, somehow, alive.* And at the funeral, Beth, at the funeral I couldn't breathe, until a ladybug landed on my collar, it did, and I knew that my mother-in-law was okay."

You are the same, Joanne, and you are different. You are who I thought you'd be, and you are not that person at all.

"I've felt confused."

"This I imagine."

"I've felt betrayed."

"I've felt that, too."

"Remember all those notes we passed?"

"Of course."

"And how we knew we would always be friends?"

"I've thought about it."

"What?"

"I've thought about friendship. How the meaning of the word will change, but not our longing for it."

My son and Joanne's son are just a year apart in age. We brought them together on the day of our reunion, a day of awkwardness, anticipation, blessings. The boys played easily together in a sunny, sodden back yard, kicked a ball around, told a few jokes, slyly looked each other over. I watched Joanne, too, and I think I caught her watching me. I wondered if that moment was a beginning or an end, the opening of the book on us or just its denouement. But none of that mattered, not really, not then. Something I had lost was found, and that was enough for a while.

2

Among Friends

ALL THE LITTLE LEGO MEN have taken their seats on the blue-green carpet. The thumb-sized horses are lined up two by two, engulfed by a patriotic retinue. The final pair of obedient beasts has been hitched to a tiny yellow basket. In the basket there's a lidless box holding a Lilliputian person — black plastic boots to his knees, a striped red shirt above his belt, a blue cape flung across his shoulders, a three-cornered hat pushed to his brow. Jeremy has been humming a funereal tune. James, an imaginary microphone pressed firm against his lips, is providing the solemn commentary.

"This, ladies and gentlemen, is George Washington," James intones. "A soldier. A statesman. A president. He caught a cold when he was out on his farm. Then he got sick. Then he died."

"Doo doo dee dee. Doo doo dee dah." Jeremy's voice is as low as it will go.

"George was our leader," James goes on. "We are feeling sad. When he died he told someone he didn't want a fancy funeral. He didn't want any fancy speeches. He didn't want a parade. But he was our hero. He rocked, good and hard."

"Doo doo dee dee, doo dee dah dah dee." The horses move forward. The baskets. The soldiers. The man. Jeremy has gone so baritone you can't hear the song's refrain.

"So here we are, in the middle of winter, burying George on a hill. See the water, ladies and gentlemen. See the hill. See the farm." The procession stops short, and the Lego men get down to business. As fast as Jeremy and James's hands can make it happen, the crowd gets to its feet. The basket creaks as it is lowered. George Washington rattles in his coffin, while James carries on with his remarks. We're all hanging on every word when, from the distant isle of the kitchen, the oven timer starts to wail. Pushing up off my elbows, I scramble out of the room and fly down the steps into the kitchen to muzzle the plaintive, pressing sound.

The M&M cookies, I soon discover, are no longer gourmet. I grab my Burn Guard cooking mitt from its spot above the refrigerator and make the necessary rescue. The cookies sizzle, spark, and deflate as they hit the cooler air.

It's nearly four-thirty, time for a snack. We always have homemade cookies on hand when James comes to play. He's Jeremy's longest-running friend and thus deserves the royal treatment, which in this house means cookies. Jeremy is an astute observer of the culinary delectations of his friends, and he issues his orders a few days in advance. For Kevin I'm required to stock Doritos and ice cream. For Will, at least a gallon of fresh milk. For Jacob nearly anything will do. For James we're obligated to provide not just the cookies I make but all the wonders that the grocery stores offer in those plastic, too-portable cups. Yogurt. Jell-O. Applesauce. Pudding. Neither Jeremy nor I dares disappoint.

Upstairs the funeral dirge, the lamentations, seem especially hallowed. James's commentary goes on unabated, and Jeremy's songs float, theatrical and sad. James is the melody, Jeremy the counterpoint. Theirs is an unusual duet.

Some kids are ineluctably bound for friendship; with Jeremy and James, it was in the air the first day they met. James's skin and Jeremy's eyes are the very same color—deep mahogany, bright as a coffee bean. The difference in the two boys' heights has lately widened; James, not yet nine, is nearly my height, while Jeremy comes no further than our shoulders. The boys have never, it seems to me, taken notice of the chasm. What they see is what too many adults lose the capacity to see: the fantastic, animate, utterly made-up things that zing through each other's heads. They explore the world together, as kids playing with kids always do. I'll open this door, one says to the other, if you open that one in return. And on each other's heels and urgings, they climb through tunnels and rancid piles of leaves and come out the other side: beguiled, expanded.

Three years ago, when Jeremy was newly six, and conversation and social games were not his forte, he would take solace in the cars in the kindergarten buckets, erect whole cities on the free-play carpet, get the traffic intelligently flowing. Crouching on his knees near Jeremy, James would settle in—back the Mustang out of the garage, turn it around, head it down the street in the very direction Jeremy had set the traffic going. James would stop at the stop signs, wait for the lights to turn green, respect the inevitable cul-de-sac detour where the traffic could wheel only one way. In their Quaker school on the hill, James would give their play all kinds of commentary, saying enough for the two of them, as if Jeremy's quietude were integral to the game.

All around them girls would be stringing beads and chattering six-year-old gossip, and boys would be off with boys, rough-housing like broncos or Indians. But James and Jeremy had their own choreography worked out—each trusting each to respect the rules and each other.

Some twenty miles separate the boys' houses now, and, further endangering the friendship, both boys left that Quaker campus last year and took their places in brand-new schools. Nevertheless, we make a point of hosting James, and it is always a Big Deal when he comes. As soon as Jeremy finds James standing on our porch, we're in for an afternoon of giggles. For an African safari. For a rock-and-roll band in our dilapidated garage. For the formation of new religions, new mathematics.

Everywhere children conspire to make the whole world up. It isn't just psychologists who say so; we find the truth embedded in novels, in memoirs. We find it in the work of Nobel Prize winner Elias Canetti, whose book *The Tongue Set Free* takes us back to where it all begins; he is telling our story as he tells his. "We had a lot of games and got on very well," wrote Canetti of his cousin Lauricia.

It was as if the age difference between us didn't exist. We had joint hiding places, which we revealed to no one, and we mutually collected little objects there, and whatever one of us had belonged to the other as well. Whenever I got a present, I promptly ran off with it, saying: "I have to show this to Lauricia!" We then conferred about what hiding place to put it in, and we never argued. I did whatever she wanted, she did whatever I wanted, we loved each other so much that we always wanted the same thing.

Childhood is the magic spell kids naturally cast upon each other, the naked eagerness to pitch feelings and actions to extremes. Kids together go where their parents cannot. "We were more daring on roller skates, we could run faster on our long legs, we could spit drinking water further than any other boy or girl," M. F. K. Fisher writes of herself and a boy named Red in her memoir *To Begin Again*. "Separated we were perhaps a little above average; together we were breathtaking. And I loved my glorious new life almost as much as I did Red, which was a great deal." And if childhood friends don't exist—and even when they do—children invent them, crafting playmates from thin air. "It is not a usual thing for a child to live with an invisible companion, but neither is it considered very rare, as far as I know," Fisher writes. "My brother David, who was eleven years younger than I, had a friend none of us ever saw, named Tally, and we seemed to take it for granted that although Tally was not visible to us, he was closer to David than any of us, and was therefore our important friend."

When the world starts to encroach, when responsibilities hover and differences are noticed and charted, friendship begins to assume a different hue, a more ambitious purpose. "Do you think the Quaker kids miss us?" James sometimes leans close to Jeremy to ask. "Do you think they *remember* us, Jeremy? Do you?"

"Oh sure," Jeremy answers. "Sure they do, James. They were our friends. How could they forget?"

"But they don't invite us to *all* their birthday parties," James will counter. "And they don't call me up to ask how I am."

"That doesn't mean they forgot," Jeremy tells James, laying his thin, pale arm across James's mighty shoulders to console him. "They're just busy," Jeremy promises. "They're still our friends." It's sweet and also heart-wrenching to hear the two of them talk about the rest of the world, to reassure each other that they fit in, that they've made an indelible impression. It's also a sign to me that their friendship is maturing, growing. That it is pushing out into new realms, which is a good thing, and inevitable, though of course it's laced with danger. I hope, but only silently, that they can hold on to their wonder even longer.

When Jeremy and James started at their new schools this year, they got the courage for their respective adventures from each other. On their own, they devised elaborate orientation procedures—drafting the elevations, aerial views, floor plans of their institutions and walking each other through the architecture. Together they discussed how it might feel to be new, to be afloat, to not know precisely where they were going. How would they decide whom to sit with at lunch? How would they handle all the homework? How would they break into the games at recess? How would they distinguish the bullies? At the same time, Jeremy and James jointly scripted their goodbyes to old classmates, telling the others, seriously and synchronously, that they would forget neither their faces nor their names.

Just before the school year began, Jeremy and I started making frequent visits to his new campus. We would walk up and down the shimmery halls, peering into classrooms, counting the microscopes, mildly disturbing the felt banners above our heads. We would imagine ourselves as part of that community —anticipating whatever we could, making what was unfamiliar known. We would stop and talk with the green-eyed principal about mathematics, about Mars. We would filter down to the third-grade hall and conjure images of classmates and books, study the charts and the posters, try to pick out which desk Jeremy would own. We would make feeble estimations about the qualities of his teachers and pretend we had the whole thing figured out.

A few days before the start of school, James made the campus journey with us. I walked behind the two boys while they predicted their futures, nudging each other along. *We can do this.* "Your new school's got the coolest hallways," James congratulated Jeremy unconditionally, only to be met with Jeremy's avowal, "The hallways in your new school will be just as cool, James. I betcha." A jab in the thick arm of one. A jab in the thin arm of the other. A snort and an eruption of smiles. I could have walked my son through that school for an eternity, but it was James who gave Jeremy the notion that the spackle of lustrous, outrageous, intimidating potentialities could and would be easily penetrated.

One Wednesday a few months after school had finally started, James stopped by for a visit. The boys compared notes, and it became clear after a while that although the two were now navigating hallways and assignments with ease, neither had yet pierced the stratosphere of friendships.

"It's hard to be new," James confided to Jeremy.

"Yup," Jeremy said, "but we're still friends."

"Nobody's invited me to any of their parties," James revealed.

"That's okay," Jeremy comforted. "Because we're still friends."

That day James asked for a clean sheet of paper, and I found one the width of the refrigerator. I got out the Crayolas while the boys sprawled across the floor, and soon they were lost in their artwork. Jeremy drew a picture that imagined himself playing soccer—heroically, happily, acceptedly—at recess. James drew a meticulous portrait of himself and, as he kept telling me, his best friend. Jeremy on the left side, James on the right, six top teeth and six bottom for each. James used a crayon called goldenrod to tint Jeremy's skin, a crayon called burnt sienna to tint his own. Then he drew two elaborate arrows, one connecting Jeremy to his printed name, one connecting James to James's. "I want you to have this," James told me, as he was leaving that day. "So you don't forget that we're friends."

James keeps reminding me that there are things mothers cannot do for their children. For one, Jeremy laughs differently when James is sitting in our kitchen, and his language grows more fluid, and his personality shows sparks that don't otherwise fly. James extends Jeremy's abundant capacity for silliness. James asks questions I never think to ask my son. James helps Jeremy overcome a few bad habits by pointing out, with shocking precision, just how a gesture or posture looks to him, and therefore how it may appear to others.

"Sometimes, when you're walking, you get a funny look on your face," I heard James tell Jeremy once, when Jeremy was having one of his infamous "thoughts," massive daydreams that can rise up out of nowhere and seemingly scoop him, mind and soul, away. "And then your body moves in a silly strange way, sort of like you're hanging at the end of one of those bungees." *Hmm*, Jeremy said. *Hmm*, the focus of his eyes coming back down to earth, his attention drawn back into our circle. After that, Jeremy paid more attention to his walking, to his expressions, to what happens when he gets roped up in a thought. I could say "Bungee," and Jeremy would know what I meant, so the word became a code for us because of James.

Still, I must be careful not to intrude too much, for parent-hood, finally, is about walking thin lines. About being there, available, and not being there overmuch. About fervently tilling the soil our children will grow in but not blocking their sun with our shadows. I am learning, always, how to step in, how to step back. How to celebrate what two children have without disrupting its balance.

Maybe, if James and Jeremy were any other kids, I'd draw the curtains on their elaborate funeral parlor. But there's something so exquisitely soulful about these boys, something so poignantly tender in the way they are laying our first president to rest. They might be planting a seed in the ground and soothing the soil around it. It is raining today—big, cold, sloppy drops—but the sounds coming from Jeremy's bedroom have turned the weather lyric. Scraping the last cookie off the residued tray, I consider the games Jeremy has, like an overworked scholar, been required to study up on and play. Monsters, Hide-and-Seek, Four Square, Store, Bad Guys/Good Guys, Red Rover, Tag. Childhood rituals, supposedly. The rules—or at least the logic—somehow inscribed on young brains.

But imagine being a child for whom all of that is foreign. A child for whom such concepts as reciprocity and community, parity and kinship, winning and losing, are hardly native. Then put yourself on a playground at recess or at a Sunday School picnic or in a neighborhood of rowdy kids. Put yourself there and you'll know where Jeremy has been. You'll get a glimpse of just how hard, how scrupulously, how courageously my son has had to labor to fit in. You'll feel as proud as I do that he has worked his way into the melee, that he is today, even by the world's ridiculous standards, just a regular kid capable of regular games.

But then you'll also come to understand how invaluable James is, how endearing this child who, from the beginning, reached out to be Jeremy's friend. Who crouched there as his companion. Who more than met my son halfway with his own imposing imagination and whom I, as Jeremy's watchful mother, trust implicitly—no matter what he's orchestrating.

I do not trust every child the way I trust James. I'm a hawk at playgrounds, classrooms, asphalt cul-de-sacs. I watch the interplay of friends and would-be friends and foes with curiosity, compassion, and concern—collecting, all the while, evidence of friendship at its most inchoate. Sometimes I watch because it makes me remember. Sometimes I watch because it helps me look ahead. When I see two boys collecting ants in a grass-filled, lid-punched Mason jar, I think: Woodbine. The open field. Kelly and I chasing lightning bugs through the scented ribbon of honeysuckle at dusk. Kelly and I, self-anointed heroines. Kelly and I without parents, on our own. When I see a band of boys knock a lonely child down, I think: here's a story to file for Jeremy. Exhibit A, on the power of crowds, the potential dangers of marginalization.

How much do our earliest friends really matter? How much control does a young child exert over the circle of his playmates? How much of friendship does he need and want? I never thought about any of this until I had a child of my own. Until I became aware of the frenetic coalescing of "playgroups" and infant story hours at libraries, started to hear ordinary, run-of-the-mill toddler daycares described as "schools" and "socialization opportunities" and "essential to a child's psyche." Until I remembered that it wasn't until I was five, and starting kindergarten, that I, like the vast majority of my peers, had any lasting exposure to the pleasures and pressures of friendship.

But in this culture of ours, children are expected to befriend or to "parallel play" earlier and earlier: they're required to hold their own among miniature strangers. The world is too crowded, we all have to get along, kids are pushed—but too young?—into the service of friendship. At the earliest ages friendship is not a choice most children make. Rather it is a suggestion, a utility, a place to which they are taken, a jewel they are expected to rub.

By four or five, even as early as three, self-determination begins to color friendships. The three-year-old girl, hands on her little hips, begins to name the price of her best friendship. The boy who had to play with the boy from the playgroup insists that he won't, declares that he wants to play with Jimmy down the street, whose sandbox he's seen glimmering in the sun. The girl who has steadfastly refused to share the most glamorous daycare toys finally gets her just desserts when her classmates—now equipped with sufficient reason, pluck, and language—knot themselves together in defense against the miser and, in the process, learn something novel and empowering about fidelity, politics.

At a certain age, kids start to define themselves in relationship to others, start to figure out who they want their companions to be, start to plan how they will earn their friends and hold their friends and step into the challenge of friendship. They will learn to compliment, to be kind, to invite, inquire, and listen, and, equally, they will learn to shut out, close down, judge, ignore, ridicule. Loneliness is possible, and understood. Shame is possible, and it too is understood. Every friend made and brought home (or not brought home) is a steeling of one's self-confidence or an insult to one's self-esteem.

By the time a child is eight or nine, a myriad forces are in play; perhaps too many tools are sharpened. There are the friends a parent hopes for his child, and the friends the child seems to favor. There is the drilling realization that being well liked by some entails being disliked or actively *un*liked by others. There is the inescapable reality that friendship breeds comparison: one is either inadequate or superior, a follower or a leader, peripheral or central, standing on slippery sand or upon the solidest rock.

Play is what a child does, it is a child's *job*, and friends are required, earned, available—or they are not. Friendship either comes easily or it does not. A child's self-confidence may blossom or decline; patterns of appraisal and identification creep into place. Who is invited to birthday parties? Who gets picked first for team sports? Who has a place to sit in the cafeteria, a buddy for science? Who gets invited into Sammy's treehouse? Who will be protected when angry fists start to fly, and who will muster the confidence and strength to do the protecting? When the badge of honor is called for, whom can one name as one's very best friend, and who among the crowd will return the courtesy?

Choosing a friend, choosing the right friend, is a blessing. As parents, we learn to pass our wisdom down without rudely pressing in, to guide our children toward the friendships they need and want because they alone have decided they're ready, not because we're too quickly readying them.

I hear the stamping of feet, and now the two boys are whizzing past me—James with his noisy leather workboots (untied), Jeremy with his socks all twisted, floppy. They are headed to the basement to check up on the ghost. They hadn't noticed the ghost until today, when it purportedly breathed fire at them. Their delighted screams reverberated all through the house when the discovery was made. Their laughter purled up the stairwell and gurgled out into the kitchen. I was sifting the flour when they came, grabbed me by the hands, led me downstairs into the basement, where the flue on the oil heater was sucking air in, tilting back. *There's a ghost in there*, the boys told me in chorus, then flew away—clomping, tripping up the basement staircase, racing each other across the linoleum squares, stumbling up the second set of steps toward Jeremy's Lego-studded room. Maybe the ghost gave them the idea for the funeral. When I was a kid, things were connected that way.

Listening to their goings-on reminds me of a million years ago, and my brother. With a crew cut like peach fuzz and eyes like the brightest Denver sky, Jeff was the family treasure, the pot of gold at the end of our rainbow. This is a small list of some of the things my brother could do: Write the cleverest limericks. Identify every found bug by both genus and species. Whistle any tune, his pitch perfect. Jeff knew all the words to all the songs from the eternal production *The Music Man*. He could name the stars visible with his bare eyes alone, not to mention the stars he trapped in his telescope. He could speak in pig Latin faster than most Americans speak English. He could decipher any code on any cereal box in seconds flat. And Jeff was never satisfied with merely riding a bike. He rode a bike while juggling while doing long division in his head.

When I was ten and Jeff was twelve, or maybe I was eleven and he thirteen, his very best friend was a kid from across the creek and up the street, a red-headed boy named Mike G. With his broad band of freckles and fractious spill of curls, Mike had a bit of *Mad* magazine about him, though I hasten to add that he was many more parts amusing than mad. For Jeff, it was always a good time when Mike was over. They played marbles and card games and marathon Monopoly; conducted cookie-eating tournaments in between games of croquet; pored over the *Guinness Book of World Records* in search of the gal with the longest fingernails, the fattest baby ever born. Whenever I was around, I could hear Mike and Jeff together—slipping powders into test tubes, scrambling up the tallest trees, pushing ancient pennies inside sleeves of coins. They had a friendship like Jeremy and James's, and what is touching, as I look back, is that they opened it up and let me in.

My mind hasn't locked on this image for years, but as I stand here sudsing bowls and scraping goop off trays and listening to Jeremy and James, I am transported back to that mint-colored house in that suburban neighborhood. I find myself plunked down in an immense family room with (if memory serves me) a mural of a cityscape painted on its longest wall. If I look to one corner, I see Monopoly gear—the pretty paper money, the little metal hat and dog and shoe, the houses piled up on Broadway and Park Place, a handwritten sign: DO NOT DISTURB. Near the game of Monopoly is a boat of a couch with split red piping—a beat-up divan drawn out from the window to serve as a stage. Upon its cushions I once stood to sing while Jeff stood to act while our little sister, Janice, danced. I sang to "Windjammer," Jeff sang to "Trouble," Janice danced to Sandler and Young.

In front of the couch, in the center of the room, in the midst of my memory stands a wobbly, speckled collapsible table—site of magic shows and Hang Man, Crazy Eights and trivia, vast piles of pennies that needed sorting. I remember sitting there as one of three, being treated as an equal. I remember that Jeff shared Mike with me while Janice played with her friends down the street, and my mother, ever watchful, around the corner, baked her famous sandwich cookies. She was, I imagine, feeling that all was in its place. Her children were anchored in friendships, at least for the moment. They were discovering the world, finding good ghosts and bad, preparing themselves for the future.

"Are the cookies done?" the boys call to me, and before I have a chance to answer, they're in the kitchen, gusting with giggles, breaking into my reverie. I find the best six cookies on the rack and divide them up onto two plates; I walk everything over to the table. Beside me, the boys can't walk a straight line, can't stop laughing. They've started some new Lego game, and they're spasmodic with the details. Neither gets out more than a burst of three words before collapsing into nonsense and more titters. Like two drunken sailors, they sloppily take their table places, while I, shaking my head, go back across the room to get milk. When I return with their glasses, James—waving his great hands dramatically—gasps that I'm invited to their snack time. "We gotta tell you," they both keep saying. "We gotta tell you what we did." But that's all they can sputter. That's all the details for now. Whatever it is, it's clearly too good for words. I pull out the chair and sit down to join them, and I can't help myself; I, too, go helpless. Laughing at what, I could not tell you. I'm just honored to be a guest at their table.

3

Reaching Out

THE OTHER DAY I was teaching books and words to a small collection of young adolescent girls. There was a horrible cold rain outside, and we had congealed as a group, the only benefit, it seemed, of such bad weather. A languid gray had cast itself about the room. Chairs were pulled close together in a huddle. The discussion curled in all directions—threading through books the girls adored and didn't, the habit of journal-keeping, language that separates and language that heals. But beyond all that I was observing how the girls spoke to one another, how they spoke *of* one another. I was trying to discern the friendships that I sensed were rounding out that room, to calculate what had brought which of the girls together, and how deep their friendships had gone. I noticed notes being passed between two girls in the back. Two others exchanged raised eyebrows. As the hour wore on, a certain courage overtook the group. I deliberately spoke less and less, and the girls spoke more and more.

After a while it occurred to me that the girls had started boasting. Not about themselves, not really. They were boasting about each other. A fine-boned, pretty girl was leaning forward, earnestly, imploring me to read her friend's short stories. "They're so good," she was saying. "Oh, God. You wouldn't believe them. She's going to be famous for sure." I glanced around to locate this writer-friend and realized that a heavy, awkward girl was blushing. Her hair was black, long, parted hastily down the center. She pulled it closed like a pair of curtains. Her pleasure at having been identified was as ripe as her awkward embarrassment.

"Is she speaking of your talent?" I asked the dark-haired girl, after concluding that her delight was bigger than her dismay.

"I guess so," she said. "Yeah," shooting a grateful-but-I'm-going-to-kill-you look back toward the delicate girl in the front.

"Oh!" Another hand shot up. "Oh! I know something."

"What's that?" I asked.

"It's Molly," the hand waver declared. "She just had a poem in the local newspaper."

"Terrific," I encouraged, nodding to both of them, Molly mortified and shy, the hand waver emboldened and loud.

"Yeah," the latter said. "I'm the one who told her she should submit it. She's really good. You should read her stuff."

In an all-girl's school where uniforms are required, it's hard to tell who's different and who's the same, which is, of course, the point. But even as a visiting instructor, I could see how polar personalities had come, spectacularly, together. How the talent had been scooped up by the one who recognized talent, the self-effacing poet by the vivacious publicist. Such friendships may seem like the most unstable of polymers, but something actual and residual is born of them. One girl learns the majesty of language. Another learns the power of self-esteem. And whether or not the camaraderie survives, the lessons are there for the keeping.

Friendship carries one beyond oneself; this is something I want Jeremy to know. I want him to have that curiosity, especially as he looks toward his teenage years. I want him to seek out, or readily accept, friendships with people who are not precisely like him; to build an expansive, reverberant circle. To adventure out of himself through the people he meets and take them on adventures with him. But there must be in all this safety buffers, too—so that he doesn't get hurt and doesn't get stuck, doesn't experiment his way toward irremediable troubles. The more a child moves toward independence, the harder parenting becomes. The questions loom large, the answers seem puny. We have to rely on what we see and what we remember. We have to choose the right stories to tell.

Some of the sweetest evidence of our humanity comes from stories about friendships between unlikely souls. Think of *The Old Man and the Sea*, in which a young boy, Manolin, and an old man, Santiago, take care of each other's hungers. Out on the boat, fighting the marlin alone, Santiago is kept afloat, in so many ways, by returning thoughts of the boy: he misses him, imagines conversations with him, trusts that Manolin, back on shore, has not lost faith. As the voyage ends and Santiago returns home, his marlin stripped to an architecture of bones, it is Manolin who finds him, nurses him, grieves publicly for Santiago's losses—but not in Santiago's company.

"Now we fish together again," Manolin tells Santiago as the story closes.

"No. I am not lucky. I am not lucky anymore."

"The hell with luck," the boy says. "I'll bring the luck with me."

"What will your family say?"

"I do not care. I caught two yesterday. But we will fish together now for I still have much to learn." *You still have much to teach me*, Manolin says, to an old man who has lost a devastating battle at sea. And the old man wants to believe, starts planning ahead because of, for the sake of, the boy.

Unlikely friends allow each other to dream on, to rearrange or appropriate the world in ways those outside their circle can neither grasp nor affect. Differences may stack up tall around them—class, age, religion, race, gender—but something bigger than all that makes them safe and strong in the other's company. Truman Capote's stories are filled with lovely discrepant friendships between old ladies and young boys, companions with little in common save a neediness and an imagination. In *The Grass Harp*, the eleven-year-old narrator, orphan Collin Fenwick, goes to live with two older women, one of whom, Dolly, has the capacity to liberate his world. "Once a week, Saturdays mostly, we went to River Woods," the boy tells us.

For these trips, which lasted the whole day, Catherine fried a chicken and deviled a dozen eggs, and Dolly took along a chocolate cake and a supply of divinity fudge.... Catherine felt no love for the tree-house; she did not know, as Dolly knew and made me know, that it was a ship, that to sit up there was to sail along the cloudy coastline of every dream. Mark my very words, said Catherine, them boards are too old, them nails are slippery as worms, gonna crack in two, gonna fall and bust our heads, don't I know it.

Dolly and Collin have a secret that Catherine is incapable of sharing. They are as different as two people can be, yet, safe inside a sustaining friendship, they've imagined a world.

Capote's characters feed each other, nourish each other's differences. They take me deep into fiction and back to a time before my son was born. To a former neighborhood and the kids next door, with whom I fell in love. The girl was seven and the boy was five, and they were at my door before I had even moved into my house, a warm loaf of raisin-studded bread in their hands. They delivered the parcel and, shy, slipped away. Through the windows I watched them trickle down my warped marble stoop and along the sidewalk, then left, up the drooping flight of stairs that took them home. I could see them scurry through their front room and disappear, then reappear in the last room of their ambling house as, giddy, they climbed up on kitchen stools.

The children became surrogates, the subjects of my photos and my poems. They were my guests for marshmallows by the fire. They lost their teeth and brought me proof. They threw dance recitals on the hump of my front lawn. They were exotic kids—their father from Korea, their mother from an interrupted line of French—and their skin was like the flesh of almonds, their hair dark, except when stroked by sun. Then paprika happened.

In spring I hung a Christmas cactus from the rafters above the porch, and in the suspense of midair, the cactus sprang from itself, a green spider on plump red feet. Finches arrived and made a nest, and when it was time, the eggs gave way to birds. I wanted the kids next door to see, wanted to share this thing with them, and when it was dusk, when the air was cool, they came to me, as my friends. I retrieved the nest and brought it low, and there was a murmur of birds, a murmur over them as well. Every dusk the children came, the birds were lowered down, there was a murmur all around. Until one night, or one morning or afternoon, I don't remember which, one of the baby finches attempted to fly. Too soon. One less bird in the nest that dusk, when the cactus was pulled down. Distraught and concerned, I spent the evening with the kids, searching the shrubs and bushes for the departed baby finch. There was no recovery at the end of so much searching, but the girl gave reassurance: the bird would live, she promised, one human being to another. Both of us like children, sitting side by side on the steps.

Now ten years have passed, and I remember those kids when I read Capote and others; I remember when I happen across their photographs. I lean in close. I touch their hair. In the photographs she is seven and he is five, and their friendship with me sparks back: alive.

A photograph is the glance of light against grains of silver, an invisibility that grows available to the eye, a negative reversed. What have we here? It is not an original question, and yet, who isn't affected by the wonder of a photo? Who hasn't gone into the album, the attic, the worn-down shoebox, and stared, mystified, at the was-ness of a life? A photograph, more than anything, is a measure of time. It is the regret: The children were young once, as I was. They were good friends of mine.

It was from the children next door that I intuited, for the first time, that I might myself become a mother. It was through them that I got in touch with the tender swell of my soul. Before I lived beside them I had lived down the road from a rug-braiding squatter and across the street from a raving monomaniac who traveled the world in pursuit of archeological scum: lumps of rotted clay, broken beads, a necklace clasp. From the rowhouse next door came the endless siren of marital warfare, and on Saturday nights my urban neighborhood was further degraded— turned into a urinal, a scene of petty crime, everything squirming behind shadows. Once, below my window, a girl snorted cocaine from the walk. Down on her belly, like a snake.

I didn't know children. Didn't know them beyond their antics in the local laundromat, beyond the safety bar of their navy blue strollers, beyond the extreme limits of an overzealous oral school for the deaf, where I volunteered my time and which I soon, in noisy protest, left. I didn't know children really, and I didn't know the lessons they embodied. At that time I could not resurrect or remember who I'd been.

Five and seven are really glorious ages; they give us adults improbable pause. They trick us into thinking that these two essential, unordinary children will go on and on in eternal smallness. That they won't become whom they must become, whom we ourselves have become before them.

So you go outside and play. You plop down in the sandbox next door and join the kids in erecting a castle. You gather them up for story hour on your stoop. You compliment them on their cowboy boots, give them extra candy on Halloween night, stop them in the street when they pass.

Is this delusion? Is it possible to be good friends with people so very different from oneself? Define friendship, and you'll see that it fits the bill: a give and a take, a teacher and a student, a continual reversal of roles.

Without friendships between unlikely players, our neighborhoods would be poorer, our communities would flake apart more quickly, there would be a worse epidemic of loneliness. Being at school would be harder than it already is. We need the oboist to share a secret with the football star, the wild one to be netted in someone else's calm. The kids of the man who has never had a job need to hang out, when they please, with the childless careerist who lives in her own quiet suspense in the house next door. Our preadolescents and adolescents need to embrace difference, take it on as if it were a voyage. Friendship isn't just the nine-year-old boy and the nine-year-old boy who have the same sensibility about ghosts and Legos and cookies. Friendship demands that we reach.

"What do you do?" I ask my therapist friend who spends so much of her time sitting in the company of the elderly that she becomes their only friend. She says that she sits down and listens, that she touches limp hands and tight fists and allows them their despair, that afterward she ushers her friends back toward desire. "What do you do, Annie?" I ask, and she says, "What I do is that I'm there." She describes, then, a patient of hers, a photographer-adventurer grown debilitatingly old. Once a month, Annie explains, she goes to his house for a slide show, goes back in time with him. " 'Here I am in the Australian badlands,' he'll tell me," she says, his own images thrown up on the wall in the lights-out room. " 'Here I am, departing for Nairobi. Here I am on the cliff where I might have fallen, had I not hung on for dear life, because I did.' " Here I am. That and this is me.

I have a friend who goes out of her way to wedge herself in with older people. She'll find them in casinos, where business sometimes takes her, and she'll charm them and cajole them and outright revel in their smarts, until, by evening's end, a star has risen. Her hosts grow alive with instruction and advice. My friend grows deeply keen to their surprise. Things unfold as they unfold, and there's a game of poker and a game of blackjack and one or two stiff drinks at the bar. There are stories, connections, histories told. A lifeline is thrown out. Soon enough my friend is relinquishing address and time, committing herself to a lasting correspondence, to a friendship—and here's the thing—that is democratic. Each looking to the other for a little wisdom, a little joy, for validation. What is it like to be young? What is it like to be old? These friendships provide answers, and comfort. "This is what you do about blackjack dealer tips," the older one will counsel Amy later, in a letter. "Lots of split pots with no action or just two players, you tip nothing. You keep your accounting clean and careful and you remember who taught you how to play."

Maybe you've seen my friend, her dark hair like an emblem against so much white in the crowd of that casino. Or maybe in the jagged streets of San Francisco you've seen her, when she's out on the town with Charlotte. My friend Amy is the sound, athletic one. Charlotte can't be missed in her cotton greens. The one walks tiptoe-slow, and the other catches up—hurrying her gadgetry along, over the crumble of sidewalk, toward the strip. "This is my friend, Charlotte," Amy will say, of her eighty-seven-year-old accomplice, and because she demands it of them, the passersby will stop and notice: Charlotte's shirt. Charlotte's scurry. Charlotte's smile. Steadfast and earnest, Amy and Charlotte will traipse in and out of thrifts until there's a victor. A white patent leather pocketbook on a bony, fragile arm—Charlotte's prayers, she'll say in her old voice, finally answered. And Amy will say that her prayers are answered, too, that no one could be any luckier with a thrift-mate. And Amy will mean it, Amy will smile; that's what her friendships are made of.

We learn from discrepancies. I learned so much from the kids next door. I learned about camping expeditions and neighborhood raccoons, about the importance of jungle beasts and the color pink, about the prance of a two-piece bathing suit and a puppy on a leash, about the width of string that effectively yanks out a tooth. I learned that five and seven are fragile numbers, that they will fall away and wilt, so that the girl, when I looked up one day and really saw her, was so much taller and not so inclined toward awe. And the boy, headed with a bucket to the creek, forgot to raise his head and say hello.

Other people's kids are not our own. They grow up while we are in their theater, watching. And sometimes they grow beyond us before we're ready to let go. Discrepant friendships don't always last. But they leave a residue.

I hold the photographs I took of the kids next door, the poems I couldn't stop writing. I hold an audiocassette in my hands of the girl reading my stories back to me, her own interpretation. I know that ten years have passed since I really knew these children, that ten years have passed since I conceived a child of my own, and that I am who I am today in part because of a friendship I was granted with a boy and a girl.

Is coming together despite obvious differences as commonplace as it ought to be among early adolescents and teens? Certainly there are barriers to overcome. So much energy is consumed by fitting in and by perfecting the shrugged-shoulder *attitude*. Anything that stands apart, that screams *I'm different*, can put a person at risk, and kids are instinctively aware of this—plan for it, defend against it, hunch their shoulders, lower their eyes. Being too good at something can be as dangerous as being hardly good enough, for difference excites both jealousy and disdain. By ten, eleven, twelve, on up through high school, kids spend so much time locating their souls and sneaking little truths into the bargain that it is hard for them to stop and cue into whatever perfectly lovely differences simmer in others.

Nevertheless, hurdles are leapt. Friendships spring up between the bully and the meek, the chess king and the cheerleader, the bookworm and the champion swimmer. Kids find each other in the oddest situations and stick around for a while. In *So Long, See You Tomorrow*, William Maxwell's masterpiece, a teen who has lived bereft of friends suddenly discovers that he has one. "To begin with, I was as thin as a stick," the narrator tells us, as background for his friendlessness.

> In any kind of competitive game, my mind froze and I became half paralyzed. The baseball could be counted on to slip through my overanxious fingers. Nobody wanted me on their team. I was a character. I also had the unfortunate habit, when called on in class, of coming up with the right answer. It won me a smile of approval from the teacher, and it was nice to see my name on the Honor Roll. It was not nice to be chased home from school by two coal miner's sons.

For a while, Maxwell's protagonist takes refuge in the skeleton of a two-story house being erected on a double lot in a subdivision; it will be his family's home when it's complete. He retreats to the site in the cool chill after school and walks through half-finished floors and up carpenter's ladders, among the day's piles of workmen's tools. One day he finds he has company, a boy named Cletus Smith, who appears out of near thin air. "I suppose I said, 'Come on up,'" the hitherto friendless narrator remembers.

Anyway, he did. We stood looking out at the unlit streetlamp, through a square opening that was someday going to be a window, and then we climbed up another ladder and walked along horizontal two-by-sixes with our arms outstretched, teetering like circus acrobats on the high wire. We could have fallen all the way through to the basement and broken an arm or leg but we didn't.

Boys don't need much of an excuse to get on well together, Maxwell's character notes. "I was glad for his company, and pleased when he turned up the next day.... We played together in that unfinished house day after day, risking our necks and breathing in the rancid odor of sawdust and shavings and fresh-cut lumber." Cletus doesn't make fun of the narrator's way of speaking. He shares the house, the open views, the envelope of quiet—making it all larger, more significant, and safe, and more bittersweet as the plot of the novella unfolds. The boys are elementally different. They are elementally the same. It's a mystery, these discrepant friendships, and yet: consider what they yield.

How do parents help their children get ready for friends who are not, in some manner, just like themselves? To go beyond the teams they're on and the habits they have and the grades they make and the cliques they're forming and to be available to diversity, Otherness? I don't know all the answers; no one does. But for now I use stories when I can find them. Stories from life, stories from books, stories that matter. I ask Jeremy himself to fashion stories about unexpected friendships. I encourage the communion of unlikely souls: the little girl in the wheelchair, who teaches Jeremy to dance; the young woman, Suzanne, who writes to him, jokes with him, kicks the ball with him in our back yard; the most talkative boy in all fourth grade, who takes a certain pride in Jeremy's quiet endeavors. And I do whatever I can to teach from my own life's example—seeking out new personalities, bringing them home, sharing them with Jeremy, letting him count the many benefits I reap. Jeremy will be a teenager soon, and much of this will be up to him. For now, while I can, I squeeze in small lessons and trust that part of him will remember.

4

Rescue

I SPEND MORE TIME at my former high school these days, watching, recalling, anticipating. At first unorthodox errands took me back, then curiosity, and then I got accustomed to just being there in the hallways of my youth. So much about the past has been eradicated, modified — the corridors and classrooms transformed by reconstruction and repair; the lolling front lawn cut down to size, the dusty bowl of the track and field relocated and tamed by plastic coatings. Only one small part of the school has not been touched by a revisionist's hammer, and there I can stand, pressing my back against the wall, letting everything waft back to me, unfiltered: the weight of my knapsack, the layout of rooms, the size of the clocks on the walls, Mrs. Sherman's medieval history, William Shakespeare during a stroke of spring sun in the thin, protective shell of Dr. Dewsnap's advanced English class. I got to read the part of Juliet when the self-effacing, emerald-eyed basketball king was Romeo. It was the closest I ever got to having a true romance with him.

Sometimes when I go back to my old high school, or when I

flip through the tattered pages of my yearbook, I'm surprised by
the number of friends the evidence suggests I had. I wonder
how I collected them all, why I let so many slip away, and why,
when I think of high school, I think first of loneliness and
Joanne. It's a distortion. *Thanks for all the talks on the hill,* one lost
friend scribbles in my yearbook. *How can I write down in five minutes all the things I feel for you?* another asks. *Who else would question my thoughts and challenge my words as you have?* And there's
Bernice, who knew I'd be a writer, who carried that torch of
faith and sent me out into the world with a mission and a
promise: *Beth, you'll grow up to be a poet, and live in Greenwich Village, and go to corner cafés and drink wine in bathtubs, and do all sorts
of avant-garde things. You'll be a great success, and I'll buy all of your
books, because I know they'll be worthwhile.*

Where is Bernice? Where are my memories of the start and
sustenance of that friendship, and of all the other friendships,
such as the one I now recall with Trayce, the wispy-haired girl
who was crushed between two buses and whose legs were never
right afterward: *You taught me the value of true friendship, Beth,
you were always there, as a friend; it's so hard to leave here and leave
you.* Closing my eyes, thinking hard, I remember at last how I finally concocted a strategy for inserting myself into the whorl of
society at high school. I remember concluding that I'd be the
one who would listen. The one who would solve other people's
problems, who would be there at moments of crisis. I'd be the
matchmaker, even. I'd bring together guys I had crushes on with
girls who deserved them, and I'd lick my own wounds alone. I
remember thinking that I'd make myself unobtrusive but essential. That I'd create a need for me. A defensive stance, perhaps,
and certainly nontraditional. But it ultimately yielded an odd as-

sortment of friends, and now motherhood requires that I understand what happened then so that I can bring perspective to my
son.

I never belonged to a clique. I was never conventionally popular. I was not, in the end, invited to those smoky basement parties, into teenage danger zones, to tribal convocations, the parties *after* the parties, where the worst and best of things
happened. I wasn't a teen like that; I lived a different, protected,
family-centered life. At school I listened to whoever wanted a
listener—in the library pit, on the grass out front, near the
lockers in the hall. I helped the unhappy girls work out their
troubles and helped boys pick out gifts for their girlfriends—
stationery, I remember, a little silver heart. The geniuses came
to tell me of difficulties in PE, and the runners asked for help
with algebra, and somewhere along the way I was more than
useful, I was liked—quietly, by individuals, steadily, without
fanfare, not enough to be included in parties, but enough to be
greeted warmly in the hallways. I don't think I realized until
high school was long over how many people, besides Joanne, relied on me for something, how many people I gave something
to, and gave it very gladly.

Most teenagers, it seems to me, spend a great deal of time
defining themselves in relative degrees of opposition to the status quo. Within the shelter of their clans, they're free to shake
down different postures, try on nouveau looks, sound out credos
and frustrations and ideas, declaim against parents and authority. A lot of conforming to nonconformity goes on, a lot of us
against them. Risks are taken and defended or disguised, and
much of what goes on is supremely volatile, capable of disintegrating beneath the fuzzy weight of whispered rumors, slim be-

trayals, the machinations of popularity and image. And all the while they're auditioning parts of themselves and evaluating aspects of others, teens are playing, just being kids, grabbing their skateboards and mountain bikes, tapping into chat rooms, planning practical jokes, turning their broadening backs on the growing inevitability of adulthood and all the heartache and responsibility it brings.

In the high school now, in the course of just hanging out, I've gotten to know a group of five boys. One is an athlete and one is a philosopher and one is an artist and one is searingly, vociferously smart; the fifth is brainy, too, only in subtler, less aggressive ways. These five kids have been the best of friends for years. They take their strength from one another. They announce their politics together; the school identifies them as a group, a single organism. They have a public, to-be-reckoned-with persona. You can find them in a handful of places—in the high school's TV studios, filming farces or Claymation; in the empty after-school hallways, whooping it up over laser tag; at the midnight showing of the latest science fiction flick; sprawled out across the floor at one another's houses. They're together, always, and yet they guard one another's individuality, pointing out in conversations with me that what unites them above everything else is their willingness to respect each other's nonconforming ways. *We're just exactly who we are,* they tell me. *There's no pressure when we're together to be anybody different.* To me these kids represent the best of everything. They have the sort of friendship I hope Jeremy someday finds; they give their differences a happy, playful home.

I wasn't a regular adolescent, and perhaps no one truly is. I worked on the periphery, the empty spaces between cliques, the private hush of sobriety. I stood at the center of no clan. I did no alcohol or drugs, did not go beyond what was expected. I stood awkwardly on the threshold of adulthood, full of counsel and theory and an eerie competence: I wasn't cool by any stretch of the word. But I listened and was thoughtful and could always solve a problem, and I knew more about many of my classmates than their very closest party friends did. It was a compromise, the best I could do. I was both necessary and forgotten, usually at the same time.

After school and on weekends, when I wasn't with Joanne I was either skating or alone. I spent most my time in the basement of my parents' home. It had a Ping-Pong table, my Uncle Lloyd's oil paintings, a not-to-be-opened closet door behind which Christmas presents stacked up all year long, and, best of all, a clunky stereo system encased in faux wood paneling, over which I had authority. The first record I ever owned was a Jim Croce album, which—I'll never forget this—was my father's purchase, presented to me one Saturday morning before anybody else was awake. I took Jim Croce down to the basement and played him till his grooves were nearly flattened. With money earned from tarring the driveway or weeding the garden, I went on to acquire Elton John and Billy Joel, James Taylor, Dan Fogelberg, Carole King, Boston—records first heard in Joanne's bedroom. I knew every song on every album, I privately sang and danced to them all. I'd come home from school, grab something to eat, call Joanne, and go down to the basement. And when I was down in the basement singing these songs, I was aware that I was alone, that the friends I had at school were off with their braver, more daring, unfettered friends, exploring secret things in secret places in the cavernous hours after class.

I put on Elton John as loud as he would go and I danced. I sat on the cold linoleum floor and put my soul in the hands of James Taylor. It was easy to feel sorry for myself, imagining all that was going on without me. I'd hear the talk about last Saturday's party, or about this coming Friday, when Sally's parents would be away. I'd hear outrageous tales about sex in closets, about liquor raids, about guys who never made it home. I realized that an entire sea change could occur at one outing, and when Monday came I'd sift through the wreckage, the secondhand news, and try to understand the world as it had come to be, the problems that would now be winging my way.

My mother must have seen what she could see, must have worried. She must have wondered why I was not often invited out, or perhaps it's safe to say that she did not wonder; she knew there was a price to be paid for my rigid adherence to childhood codes, the responsibility I felt to be *good*. She must have known, in my sophomore year, that I was dreading my birthday. That it had become a symbol, in my own anxious mind, of the friends I couldn't invite to a party, the friends I wasn't sure I really had.

That year, that birthday, I remember having cake, opening presents with Joanne and my family, then going down to the basement, feeling unpopular and somber. I remember turning on the lights and lowering Cat Stevens onto the turntable and turning around and looking up and realizing that I was facing a crowd. The tall, green-eyed captain of the basketball team. The guy I'd tried to flirt with at the bus stop. A cheerleader and a few ice skaters and the class president. The guy who called me Bellen, the guy whose gift was origami, the captain of the swim team, a math nerd, a drama queen, Trayce, a long-distance runner, and, of course, Joanne. I did not know then and I cannot to this day imagine how my mother did this. How she knew who they were, how she convinced them to spend my birthday with me. Except for the endurance of my marriage and the beauty of my son, nothing since has so thoroughly surprised me. For my Sweet Sixteen my mother gave me a raft of friends, and I floated with them, happy.

Who will I be for Jeremy, if friendship grows fugitive for him? How will I know when to intervene, and what gift I can give? I was in California last week, at the house of a dear friend, at a party. I had never been there before, never known how my friend lived—among so many thousands of read books, among so many photos and frames, at the very top of the seashell-colored hills of San Francisco. I had not imagined the authors she keeps piled by her bed, or the tiny table where she writes, or how within the slimmest alley of a kitchen she cooks up pork roasts and Dr. Seuss–style cakes and manages—I should say *orchestrates*—all the pots and pans on the wall, all the oranges in their blue netted bag on the floor. I hadn't imagined all that my friend, Kate, can do, and I hadn't imagined her son. Not his whole self, not really. I hadn't imagined beyond the freckles she'd told of, beyond the two-shades-of-green frog I know he once captured, brilliantly, beyond the worries I knew he sometimes had at school, as very smart and sweet kids on the edge of teenagehood tend to have. They need to know they have a place in the world. They need someone to show them.

So there was Kate's son, late on a Saturday night, in a huddle with his friends, maybe eight or nine of them, watching a James Bond movie. They had broken into the pizza boxes and the apple cider, the blue plastic plates, the blue paper napkins. Their fraying, graying socks were everywhere, their slouches, their elbows, their knees, and inside a room of books they were lobbying for space with the presents. It took my heart, took me by surprise. It reminded me of my sixteenth birthday and threw my thoughts ahead. The boys in one room, and Kate and her husband and their little, blue-eyed, awestruck girl just one room away—everyone safe in the house that Kate had made, and Kate's son, I suspected, the safest of all. His friends had come, and he was there with them. He could float on their raft for a while.

5

After Thoughts

IF A PHOTOGRAPH is a measure of time, a letter is a measure of the heart. In my house there are far too many letters. They unfold like the bellows of an accordion in the muted attic light. Once I saw an image of a man and a tsunami. April 1, 1946, Hilo, Hawaii. The man stands on a pier while the titan wave hurls itself at him. His arms are crossed, his back is straight and upright, and in this, the very last instant of his life, he will not cower. He looks into the eye of the sea, not running from that which there is no running from, just standing there, meeting the storm.

I have no such bravery. Not, for certain, on the unprotected shore, and not in my attic, which reduces me to half my height and heavies its dust into my lungs. The letters here are a life and a condemning, the better half of so many startling conversations. The letters are my mother loving me through college, my uncle joking me from sadness, a boy, a girl, a jilted friend asking, *Why? What did I do? Where have you gone? Will you return?* The letters here are a mirror, and who can bear facing it all again? Who really wants to acknowledge: *I played a part in this.*

If my mother's letters wrench me with emotion, the letters of a neighbor wreck my sense of self. There must be hundreds here, on onionskin paper, all black loopy ink save one bright banner of red. In the Bibles of the house I find her letters, and inside the clamp of cookbooks, and in whatever I was reading when they arrived. They came here with me five years ago, after we moved some distance away from her. Proof, if anyone needs it, of what friendship can provide.

Her children were the ones I borrowed, and her house was but two strips of driveway from mine—two lumpy splats of asphalt and a burst of thorny weed between, a patch of utter depravity that would never pass for a garden, which she claimed because I wouldn't. We shared a tree in the back, and a bit of fence gnawed our property line. I had a city job and was childless when our relationship began. For one reason or another, she felt compelled to bring me food. Extras of the Korean dishes she concocted for her husband, an enigmatic man who slept past noon and hardly said a word I understood. I never took the time to know him well.

I understood her, though—she had the slyest sense of humor —and I loved her dark-haired boy and girl. And while my habit of writing was not something I typically divulged to strangers, I did one day write a poem about her kids and think, an after thought, to slip a copy to her.

Our mailboxes were nailed directly to our houses—creaky rectangular metal-hinged things, lined up even with the door- bells. On this street privacy wasn't part of the bargain—every colorful carpenter-style house a stone's throw from the next in the row, most moms home for their children, porches and stoops and playthings all communal property. Trains rumbled through the depression of our back yards so routinely that we set our clocks by them.

Nevertheless, amidst all the busyness and busybodies, Andrée, within hours, surreptitiously slipped a note back to me. The envelope small as a drugstore valentine, the contents folded twice timidly, on airmail paper. This, the only letter that I cannot now find, began a daily correspondence between neighbors. I answered her with another poem. She answered with a torrent of encouragement. Back and forth, back and forth, the ground rules somehow establishing themselves, the notes couriered, always, in the dark, down the sidewalk, up the steps, across the porch floorboards, on very quiet shoes, for six portentous years.

Think what you will, this was essential. This is what I needed more than my sleep, which I began, in increments, to sacrifice. It is true, I had been writing all my life, but writing for no one. Now there was Andrée, more intelligent than one could imagine, more adept at breaking the lines apart and giving them back, rejuvenated. She would wait for whatever was coming next and make me believe that it was important.

The irony—and of course there was irony—was that the analysis was always infinitely smarter than the object that had provoked it. I assure you, it is fact: Andrée's commentary dancing on the sharp blade of brilliant, my poems pulled from a bucket of slop. There is no false modesty here. There is—looking back on it—the antecedent of something like shame. I was given more than I deserved, and I took it and took it, for years.

. . .

What do we need friendship for, once we're free and clear of schoolyard bullies, high school cafeterias, adolescent identity crises, simpleminded play? Once we're out on our own and besieged by distractions, why do we still yearn? Why do we spend time making and keeping friends and remembering to remember friends and praying that our friends will miraculously remember us?

Adult friendships are not the same among women as among men; women talk, the cliché says, while men revel in mutual doing. Of course friendships between men and women are of an entirely separate sort, and some friendships defy any kind of code. No one relationship looks like any other, and even two individuals, when joined by a third, change their modus operandi, their defining point of view.

I have friends today who hold me in their circles — friends from church, from the neighborhood, the mothers of friends Jeremy has brought home from school. I have friends from the magazines I write for, from the companies that once employed me, a friend here and there from my college days. Each circle of friends is a support, each calls upon and sustains in me a different melody; depending upon the company I'm keeping, I am only a mom, or only a writer, or only the neighbor with the biggest pile of leaves. My friends have enabled me to become a woman, and I am a woman because of the friends I keep — because of the way I look for Lori and Lori looks for me in the lobby of Jeremy's school, or the way, when I'm sick, Kathy bakes me her lasagna, or the way I can call Jamie anytime I'm stuck for a recipe. I am who I am because of the way Tom listens, because of the truths that Ken makes, because Susan never lets me get away with my exhausted second best. I am who I am because my friendships keep on growing—because there are always new people slipping into my life, new voices, new stories, new faces I look for, new homes that open up to me.

Out of high school, out of college, our friends come to us in waves: at work, in the library, at parent-teacher nights. Some of these friendships are massively important, and some simply get us through the day. I've drawn the conclusion that taken together they help us feel more whole. They succor us, they fill in the blanks, they give us a purpose. Because all friendships are finally mirrors, they provide proof that we do exist, that we are. Friendships root us deep into the earth, find us our water when we're thirsty. They give us a reason to laugh as well. To just laugh at life, flat out, and keep on going.

We all look for different qualities in those we seek as friends. At twenty-four, two years out of college, engaged to a guy who lived hours away, free at last of any roommate, what I wanted most was a way to pass the time. I wasn't watertight and I knew it; I was perpetually wavering on my own edge, looking for ways to keep myself moored while I waited for my boyfriend to return. I'd managed to fall in love with a guy who wasn't around, who hadn't a phone, who sent watercolors instead of words—and who would become my husband nonetheless. I felt held in suspense and also crimped shut—uninterested in hanging with other women my age in the sour singles bars, insufficiently independent to trek to movies alone, still possessed of enough common sense to avoid crashing in on other couples. Seeking escape, I turned my energies to a brand-new job. Here, I said, I'll make my friends. I'll establish my base, earn my place, be encouraged, brought out, become whole.

In remembering friendship, one necessarily trips back and back and remembers the humiliation of its opposite.

To get to my place of employment—a design firm housed in a riverside warehouse—I had to walk halfway across town: a straight shot up Locust Street, fifteen easy city blocks. I lived on Camac Street then, in a row of townhomes whose tenants were the victims of the architecture's charms. The houses were narrow, three stories tall, and in those that had been divided into apartments the interiors were consumed by stairs. I lived in a single room on the second floor of an alley-hugging structure, an unwelcome climb up steep, tremulous stairs whose blood-colored carpet was alternately stained brown or whited out to bare nubs. When you opened the door to my minuscule room you saw it all—the bed, the bookshelf, the hot plate, the palm-sized TV. That room was my study, my living room, my dining room, the place where I laid my body down and tipped my head back so as to salute and root on the moon. I could see across the alley into the back room of my neighbor. I knew what she wore, I knew when she read. I knew about her coffee after dinner, about the crumbs she threw to the pigeons, about how she stripped to her underwear, a towel laid across her breasts, to sunbathe on the black iron fire stairs. I never once saw her out on the street, and I never waved hello.

Camac Street was where I acquired the habit, which I've never since quit, of getting up long before dawn. I seem to be attracted to absolute stillness, which you can get at that hour of the night. Or, rather, what you get is the differentiation of sounds, so that you can hear the lid of the trash can fall and the swish swish of the cat denying its crime. You can hear the clock's second hand move from one tick to the next tock, and the sound of your heart, and the sound of your breath, and the sound of the pen across the page, the sound of a story moving forward. I liked that hour of the night, but I also felt caged—no one to talk to, nowhere to go, no way to even pace the floor, my husband-to-be in a school far away, swamped with friends and an exhilarating purpose, where he was, without question, moored, and often, or maybe just sometimes, at risk of forgetting me.

So I left for work early. I started as soon as the veil of darkness had lifted and I was sure that I wouldn't be alone among the homeless, the prostitutes coming home from the job, the city sweepers warming their hands above the grates. I got to work early, and I brought not just my hired writing skills and my glancing knowledge of design but a fantastic faith that I would soon be in the circle of an established work family.

My optimism was not, as it turned out, either reciprocated or rewarded. It wasn't that I didn't excel at my job, because, with a bombastic valor, I did. I volunteered for every project imaginable, and I did whatever I could snatch up to do with speed and a jinxy competence—writing clever biographies of the firm's principal designers, fashioning cliffhanging descriptions of the firm's most important structures, researching obscure marketing leads, writing passionate theses on why the firm should enter the health care market and steer clear of retail. At one point I even took on the writing of a massive monograph on the firm's forty-year history, which I worked on at night for more than five months, never asking for or even wanting an extra dime. Everything I did then stemmed from a desire to be recognized, a need to be liked, a compunction to make daylight friends to counter the austere loneliness of night.

Thinking back on it now, I understand how much I had in

common with the cat who steals the goldfinch from a tree and expects his owner to appreciatively raise the mangled remains to the skies. In my blind eagerness to earn my way into friendships, I trampled over years of standing schedules, standards, processes, approaches. I rammed right through what had been Celia's system and Maureen's philosophy and Gia's output and Frank's final stamp, thus upping the ante for the firm's marketing department. From the cluster of their desks my workmates guardedly watched me, and in hallways and Xerox rooms they whispered, and every day, precisely at noon, they left, without me, for lunch. Once, I was told, I could not use the bathroom. A meeting was held, and I was not invited.

Work became a dread, worse than the night. For every offering I sent up, there was news of someone's ruined pride, somebody else's undermining. For every outreach, there was a barricaded bathroom. *I'll do that*, I kept suggesting. *And I'll take that on as well. Let me do that, so you can go home early.* Hoping, always hoping, that I could somehow prove my earnestness, my reliability, could buy my way in. I performed these maneuvers for many months, but nothing ever cracked the shield the others had thrown up. I had wanted, needed, overtures, the whole rare human sound of encouragement. But what I got instead was the muffle of antiwelcome, the sputter of simple friendship denied. It was an unhappy time in my life, to be sure, and I have never forgotten its lessons.

This, I read now, from an old recovered letter from Andrée, *is why we need poets. It is satisfying to see our half-conceived amorphous thoughts given shape so beautifully, our experiences read back to us — first, so that we may see; second, so that we might gain insight.*

So it is, I thought then, though now, her faded letter in my hand, I merely shake my head and wonder. Hurrying to prove Andrée right, I'd prepare something rash and new, something that would elicit a penetrating response, which I then would read by the light of the moon, having brisked down the midnight hallways and out onto the porch where her letter waited. I would read and—absurdly—I would believe: *Reading this I was almost frightened by all the worlds inside your head,* she wrote. *I've heard that in professional acting there are two ways to deliver a line — by working on the elocution as an end to itself, or by working on becoming the character and letting inflection and movement flow out of that deeper place. I am sure you are of the second variety.*

Criticism came, too, but in such a gentle, roundabout fashion that only now, my ego tempered, do I recognize her stealthy reproofs: *Picked up a thin book of C. S. Lewis's poetry in church, read a few and decided his gift lay in writing children's stories,* began one letter, a few days after I'd stuffed some singsong exercise into her box. *The poems were clever and all, erudite, and even full of deep insight, I'm sure, but they RHYME so. And I can't help wondering at the sacrifice of precision, the compromise necessitated by so strict an adherence to form. And besides: they are not beautiful.*

It went on like this. *I didn't understand your whole first paragraph, but it was great,* she decided, and then: *I had to read it four times before I got your meaning, but the meaning was well worth the wait.* Increasingly she rendered the exchange of letters as an event, so that I learned not merely of their impact but of their journey back and forth between us: *I wonder how often history has been changed by acts of God like this — the wind mischievously lifting an envelope out of the mailbox and hiding it in the netting of a neglected soccer goalpost, to be discovered this morning. Now I am in the coolest spot in this whole town, and in the only block of free time I can foresee for some time to come. So here, in the wagon, in the shade, my feet planted in ankle-deep water, I revel in your piece and write.*

Over time my poems burst into fiction, and the fiction reverted to truth, and Andrée read every word. *What magic lamp do you rub to be able to remember your true stream of consciousness reactions to every unfolding incident, in the right chronological order,* she wondered, making me wonder. *Did you really see that scene with the boys in the courtyard? It fits so well with the story that I will forgive you if you didn't.*

She was my reader of one. She was the world outside my house long after I had left my city job and settled into wifehood, deep into mothering my own young son. There Andrée was, with her bits of wisdom and her Korean platters, standing on my front stoop. There she was when I lost myself in my son, his life, his happiness, all of which I started writing down. *I would come to visit,* she wrote one night, *if you weren't so far away.*

What is it that separates the woman from the cat, the man from the dog, the child from the frog down at the creek? It isn't tools (think of the birds carpentering their nests). It isn't language (for monkeys, too, have their signs). It is, I've come to believe, our willingness to hover under a lonely kitchen lamp and read, and consider, and imagine ourselves in other lives. It is compassion. And because, increasingly, I could not sleep, because our homes were but two strips of driveway and one spit of thorns apart, because I stood like a shadow at the window every night, I suddenly saw and equally suddenly understood that Andrée, out of a love for me, had become a storyteller too. When all the world was asleep I could sometimes see her, pitching up the gemstones of her life, putting her history on paper, tiptoeing out beneath the stars in an old housecoat to leave me something to hold on to in the night. Andrée started writing me stories because she knew that no one survives on their own tales, alone.

I have decided that I don't know enough words, Andrée began one night, to set my readerly expectations straight. *The only words I have for colors, for example, are the ones I knew in first grade. Maybe if I had paid more attention to my school subjects I could make interesting sentences. I do remember from geometry class what a hypotenuse is, and I'm still waiting for a place to use it. It's not a very pretty word though. Sounds like a lumpy animal related to rhino.*

But of course she blew her cover soon. *I love my mother, and I think she is a better mother of 40 year olds than four year olds, but I can remember only one time in my childhood when she ever varied her cleaning routine, made the smallest crack in the rigid, self-appropriated role she cast for us both — it was one morning, I might have been four or five, when she took me in from playing outside to teach me a French song on a Harry Belafonte record. I would have loved for her to wake me to see the moon.*

Followed by this story, which ran up my spine then as well as now, as I reread it by the lamp of my flashlight: *My first and only noteworthy event in forty years came when I won the canned goods raffle: 300 students in the school all hearing my name over the intercom system at the same time. I had brought in the one can of Campbell's soup and so had only one slip of paper in the big barrel in the Principal's office. It was a miracle, I think, fate briefly smiling upon me against all the odds. With great ceremony, I was escorted to the office, where Soeur St. Edouard de la Croix herself handed me the prize: two tickets to see "Ben Hur" at the Stadium Theater. I had seen it before but wanted to go again, conjecturing that it would taste even more de-*

licious when it was free. My mother, however, deemed it more in con-
formity with the universal laws of fairness that my little sister Lise,
who had not seen it even once, should have her chance. It was decided
that Lise would go with Memere, and by all accounts a good time was
had by all. That is, until Lise got bored before intermission and
Memere had to take her home. Which I guess is understandable due to
the fact that she was only in second grade.

How many years did I live beside my neighbor before I could engage myself in the jumble of her hippie days, her wedding on a Korean hill, the fables of the mill town where she grew up? How many years before there was any sort of balance between the stories given and the stories received? Before the questions and answers and suggestions flowed out in both directions? Before I stopped to declare the triumph of her talent, before I said, straightforwardly, without literary disguise: *Andrée, thank you for all that.*

Looking back on the remains of those six years I am filled, like a reservoir, with regret. I am astonished all over again by what Andrée said and how she said it, and by why she steadfastly did. I read her letters, her poems, her most exquisite essays and wonder: Did I say enough? Did I praise enough? Does she know how precious she is? Does she know what her friendship meant to me, how it gave me the strength to live on? I know what it is to be denied a friendship. And I know what it is to be embraced.

It is a drowning thing to go back in time, to submerge myself in the history of the attic. And it is so dark here that I can barely see, so dusty that my lungs have begun to protest and wheeze. Yet I do not feel free to crawl away from all this, to leave a six-year correspondence in a tangle on the floor. I am searching still, for some small rescue from my own regret, some reprieve from an unequaled friendship, some proof that I earned this extraordinary neighbor's grace. In the thickened light I allow the last of her letters to filter through my hands and fall, until only one is left, a card, which I open now: a brevity. *It was a pleasant thing to see you at the door this afternoon with a big potted marigold.* I catch myself, feel the heat behind my eyes, read it slowly, again, so like redemption. *You said nothing at all.* Andrée promises this: *I'll assume that it is just because.*

6

Nesting

"IF I COULD I would build you a nest high up, on a land of trees, near where the river bends to blue."

"A nest?" I ask. It is the present time. Down the hall, behind a closed door, on the bed that was mine years ago, Jeremy sleeps. Here, in this forest-colored room, I lie with Bill. Memories are blowing like a chinook through the house, and I have pulled the bed sheets over our two weary heads to keep us safe. We are face to face; I see the spangles of his eyes. I can feel, and am desperate for, his heat.

"A nest of glass, high in the clouds, where you could see everything, always, where you could just look out and see," Bill says after a while. "And a staircase of books between the ground and the nest."

"And for you?" I ask, kissing him softly, grateful that he remembered the books. "What about you?"

"And for me, I suppose, a cave—dug out of roots and slugs and leaves, the crumble of humus," he decides, leaning back into his own reverie. "Where I could paint. And think. And rest."

"What about Jeremy?" I ask, absurdly rushing toward the details now, trying to conjure this house, trying to decide which river we'll live beside. "What room would be his?"

"It's a house without doors," Bill says, his voice fading in the darkness. "He'll run between us." Bill's breathing comes from a calm inside his chest. His eyes are closed, he has the atmosphere of sleep. In the heat of his arms, which have gone loose around me, I am aware of the wind, still in the house, blowing above the bed sheets. We have little in common, I think. So very little. The sky and the earth, the light and the dark, the height and the depth, the words and the colors, and the child between us. Little in common, but who would I be without him?

Can you marry a man for the way he paints? For the stories he tells? For his mysteries? Can you base the decision on something like faith? How many facts do you need?

I have friends of both sexes who speak of settling down the way others might speak of choosing a wardrobe. They simply tried on a number of partners for size, and finally, like a glass slipper, one fit. Other people fall in love with a person as they might fall for a religion—without stopping to measure or analyze, without systematically screening and filtering and testing for proof of long-term compatibility. I fall into the second camp for sure. At twenty-three, having turned down several marriage proposals from some all-too-suitable men, I gave my heart away to an enigma, a dark-haired man with capable hands who dreamed in, and softly sang, a different language.

It would have been simpler, I used to think, if I had never happened on those paintings in that West Philadelphia room where Bill lived with a guitar, a trestle table, pans and crinkled tubes of color, ox-hair brushes, a broken, lunging chair. There was a mattress in one corner, a hot plate in the kitchen. There were paper towels and linseed oil in the pantry, where cans and cartons of food should have been, and there were watercolors drying on the deep, vast windowsill.

You can't imagine what it is to hold a painting that tells you everything there is to know about a man. Or perhaps you can. Perhaps you have been there, too, in the knock of surprise, when someone shows you something he conceived of, wanted, made. It is so much more than good. It says, unmediated: *I am.* It says, without the bore of words: *I have been.* So what do you do about that when you find a painter? When he's everything you're not, and you're in love.

We met, but he was getting ready to leave. We were in love, but in a month he'd be gone—headed to the graduate program he'd already put off for a year. *I've been in Rome,* he explained. *Singing in the subway.* He had long hair, three faded shirts, two pairs of jeans. He had a Latin face and a smattering of freckles. He washed his clothes at the corner laundromat while Tawanda, Taewiki, Raji, and the rest of the neighborhood looked on, and he had a stash of photos from the place where he was born. Black-and-whites. Thick Kodak paper. Thumbed to a thickness along every edge.

"Tell me."

"El Salvador."

"And this?"

"The coffee farm."

"This?"

"Garlic cloves. The marketplace. A beauty queen. A whore."

"And Rome?"

"I sang."

"You sang."

"I sang and I painted and I etched."

"And these, then? These?"

But about the paintings I couldn't ask him. They were drying in the moonlight, on the ledge.

The most dangerous thing I ever did before Bill was to set out walking through the city, alone. Or think about poems or want to write them. Or fail to look ahead. That was danger where I came from. That was living on the edge.

I was through with college. Out, but not really on my own, still living at home while I sought my destiny, and a little nervous, I think, that I wouldn't find it, that all the men I'd meet would be like the ones I'd already met, bound for success, status and stature and things that hold no weight for me. What do you do with the sprawl that is the life you've not yet lived? How will you know when love happens? I had been looking for something I could believe in, and there were Bill's paintings, drying still.

Watercolor is a tender, nervous medium. It both eludes precision and suggests great depth; there's no returning to the idea after it's done. The artist works toward transparency, keeping the principles of evaporation in mind, and the rag paper shivers and buckles as the brush works the pigments, the binders, the preservatives. Watercolor is the chance the artist takes. No one knows for certain what the painting will be until it dries, and then it's too late to change a thing.

But certain things are knowable about a painter's hands. I knew in an instant that Bill's were gentle. His was a hand capable of yielding cadmium geometries and men with wings and a raw sienna landscape of one thousand cobalt doors. A hand ca-

pable of catching a *campesino* in a dignified pose and bringing
Bob Dylan to the Italian tunnels on the strings of his guitar. A
hand that took my hand into itself. A hand that instinctively I
trusted.

Trusted. And this was something new, the weight and quality
of this trust. It was something extraordinary—more compelling
than the mosaic of good feeling and faith that lies at the foundation of every true friendship, so very powerful that early on I
could not name it. There was nothing traditional about Bill's appeal for me, nothing conventional about how we dated. I wrote
poems while he made art. We gave each other silence. Hours
would go by, and there we would be, taking our light from separate splinters of the moon, I with a pen, he with a paintbrush,
the sounds of the city through his window. We validated each
other's passion for art forms so private that they had no purpose
larger than themselves: poems in a notebook, paintings on a sill.

My friends were out being romanced, being feted. They were
getting dressed up for the theater, performing the rituals of the
Western mating game and calling me later with the details.
They were telling me about men who did or did not fit their bill,
going through their checklists, making comparisons, computing
the size of an acceptable compromise. Hardly any of that made
sense to me. I had found a man who shared his fragment of the
moon. A man who thought my poetry could matter.

It could have been, I suppose, just a very extraordinary friendship. We could have taken what we had and made it merely an
arrangement between artists—two people in one room, retreat-
ing. But let me go back to that thing Bill gave me—that big
loom of trust, with so many fibers. A net large enough and so
exquisitely crafted that it could catch my many shards—my

moods, my regrets, my music, my joy, the person I had been, the person I was becoming. I could be every part of me—conflicted, ambitious, self-doubting, victorious. I could dance, sit, want, give, fly, and be drowning, too, and Bill would leave his lamp on for me. He would be there, come the rain, come gray hair. He would be there, and that is what I understood then. This was friendship, of course, but it was also bigger than that. Certainly it was bigger than romance. It was the size of a marriage, and it scared me to death. I hadn't meant to fall in love with an artist.

Falling in love changes everything. It's not just your selves— one person to another—that are affected. It's all the charged particles of friendships that smoke and twist around you, an invisible, palpable force. His subset of friends plus your subset of friends, which will never add neatly together. The way each of his friends brings out unexpected sides of him, the way each of yours unspools you in ways he could not have seen coming. You need his friends to help you learn who he is, and he needs your friends to do the same. You need to know each other in a crowd, and in aloneness, and you need to trust your ability to draw lines between the two.

We had a month—one month—before he had to pack his tinny, tiny car with the tubes and brushes and pans of his trade; one month before he would be gone for a two-year stint in a city four hours north. Early on, unable to abide by better instincts, I decided that the circumstance was daunting; we should call the romance off. It felt too big—too overpowering, too impossible, too deep a chasm, too fine a web, too much of what I hadn't expected. And besides, he was going away.

The trouble was, there was no one like him. Without so much

as a conversation he had shown me the color of his soul, and then he'd started talking, telling me tales about El Salvador and the characters he'd known. Revealing the life he had lived. Back home, he said, there was a maid named Nicha, a stocky, flat-footed, pitch-black-haired woman who had given birth alone twelve times—she had lain down in the undergrowth of the jungle, Bill said, and cut the cords of her children with a blade of glass. Back home was Tiburcio, small and light-boned as a bird, who had macheted a man to death, then sat dwindling in a jail cell until his freedom could be bought. Back home was Lenora, her eyeballs blind and hard as marbles, her tortillas better than any others on the farm. There was a friend named Periquito, a barrio inhabited by gorgeous half-breeds, a bracelet of widows and divorcées who jangled around Bill's childhood home, laughing their miseries away. When a man tells you about the people he has known and the people he has passionately loved, he is inviting you into his family, bringing you into his life. He is standing above you, spreading his branches, and you are looking up at so many leaves.

Still, it bears repeating: Bill and I had nothing in common. He was a man of the world; I was naive. I read; he most assuredly did not. He drew; I had no such talent. He was Catholic; I had never sat through Mass. He had traveled far from his country, his customs, his language; I was still hovering near home. When Bill wasn't telling stories he had very little, at least in my company, to say. He liked the silence. He liked the moonlight. He liked it fine that I was just there, fiddling with words or dancing with shadows, while he bent over the color trays and painted. Here we were: two foreigners in a shambles of a room. The stuff that gets lodged in a poem.

Daylight was another country. Daylight was when we feigned an ordinary friendship for the sake of appearances at the office. This was my first job out of school, and I'd talked my way in, and basically I sorted slides, straightened materials boards, and answered requests for proposals while everyone else, including Bill, designed waterfront parks and themed shopping malls, planned rehabs, colored cartoons with squealing Pantone-tinted markers. I had wanted to be around architects and architecture, and here I was, lacking every qualification save the unqualifying fact that my mysterious great-uncle, designer of the Waldorf Astoria and other landmarks, had instilled in me a passion for sculpted space. A glorified gofer, a professional outsider, I wore short pink dresses that umbrellaed out below my waist and trotted up and down the one corridor, delivering messages, transporting carpet samples, suppressing my desire to pull Bill into the concealing hum of the dark, rank blueprint room. We'd pass in the hallway, brushing hands. I'd tuck notes into his parallel bar. He'd stick his head into my office when he and his friends were heading out. *Hoagies,* he'd say. *You want to join us?* As if it were an afterthought.

So I knew Bill two ways. I knew him as he was at night, the artist wanting nothing. And I knew him by day, as part of the hurried mix of things, the humor, as part of the ongoing debate about Louis Kahn and Frank Lloyd Wright and the interloper, Robert Venturi. Bill taking Kahn's side and fighting it till the end, J. C. defending Venturi, Mike evangelizing for Wright, everybody throwing scumbags and accusing the others of all kinds of crimes, accusing Bill until he'd start flinging the accusations right back, proving his point with hasty sketches on yellow tracing paper, dredging up proof positive from the library.

It was a good place, a good job, a safe, friendly haven after college. I got to hang out with the designers even though I couldn't draw an arc, and I was part of the crowd on South Street, the lunch hour at the dark, hot Reading Terminal, the cluster on the shallow steps of Penn's Landing, where obscure little bands would play for cheap and the water ice left our young lips blue. After work, up on the hill near Memorial Hall, there were softball games captained by the two Mikes, and no one kept score, and Bill lay braiding grass blades and telling stories that were not the stories he told me at night, the conversation sparking like the fireflies Kelly and I used to catch in our jars. Once the gang of us raided the local WaWa and headed north to overtake a lake. The volleyball game went on long past dusk, when all the coolers were empty and the lake had turned moon gold and the gnats had found some other diversion. I sat on a folded newspaper listening to stories, listening to laughter, watching Bill and loving Bill, and afraid of the feelings I had.

We had only one month, and one week of that month had gone by. Hardly enough time, yet those days stand out as the longest and cleanest in my life. Those friendships, those excursions, those scumbag fights, those Schuylkill River picnics, those volleyball games, those lakes of gold. Those midnight hours when again I had the painter to myself, the painter and the stories he gave me: El Salvador and Nicha, Tiburcio and Lenora, the beat and the pulse of the farms. When all the others were gone, Bill imagined his childhood into the present for me. I was his audience; he acted. Cicadas singing in the street, two boys drawn into a distant quarrel, somebody haplessly tuning their car by the orange street lamps, and Bill looking at me with the boats of his eyes, giving sail to the life of his grandfather.

Recounted more quietly than the rest, his eyes on the moon, these were the stories that finally let me take that leap. Bill, have I ever told you that? *My grandfather,* Bill would start. His dark eyes dampening, he would have to start again, *My grandfather...* And then he would tell the exotic tales of a man who had started out like any commoner but had died with five coffee plantations to his name. Five coffee plantations and hordes of *campesinos* who to this day remember the smell of the pipe he smoked, the way he sat on his horse, his intelligence about planting seasons and October winds. Carlos Alberto Bondanza brought the priest to the jungle to give the peasants their holy days. He insisted on fair wages. He opened his huge white city house to his unbridled grandchildren, was the center of calm during earthquakes. He was the most important person Bill will ever know. He is the central fact of my husband's life.

He took me to Rome when I was fourteen.

He read me the comics before I could talk.

My first memory is him, outside, the sound of his voice.

How much does someone need to tell you before you know the stretch and the smell of his soul? When a man opens to you like a page in a book, opens with all poetry and heart, watching the moon, telling the truth, there's no not loving him. There's no not looming him into your web. There is no going back. This is what is true about the life I chose to live: Bill is the most dangerous thing I've ever done, and he is also, as time has proved again and again, the safest and smartest and dearest. He is my best friend and also my lover, and he's the artist he always was, his paintings in a scatter on our sills. We are here because trust is, because it has saved us from ourselves.

"We're not saying goodbye," Bill promised me on the last day of August in that year, 1983. His car was packed. He was headed north. The garret in West Philadelphia was stripped and empty. They had already said farewell at the office, thrown him a party at the lake.

"Are you really coming back?" I asked. "Give me a sign. Give me some proof." *Give me something that will break this trust, or give me something that will hold it.*

"I'm coming back."

"Prove it."

"Believe me," he said. "You have to believe that I'm sticking with you. That I plan to stick around." He looked at me and kissed me then on the tears that clung high on my cheeks.

"Maybe you won't need me. Maybe you'll find out you won't."

"I'm going to be there," he promised. "I'm going to wait around until heaven. I'm going to be there when you and my grandfather finally meet."

I'm going to be there. When you and he meet. I'm going to wait around until heaven. He was talking about his grandfather. He was talking about me. Both of us there, in one place.

Beside me now, Bill is soundless while he sleeps. His hand rests light as silk below my breast, and his freckles stand in acute relief against his skin. A nest of glass, I think. A cave carved out of dirt. An exceptional child between us. We have struggled in this marriage, Bill and I, and yet we are still here, fifteen years on. Tied by the things we cannot see and by things we just imagine. Our stakes are steadfast in the ground, weathering the seasons of our marriage.

7

Back Home

LAST SUMMER Bill's grandmother called him home, where he had not been for five years. We had stayed away because of what El Salvador had become in the afterclap of war. Because of too many guns in too many idle hands. Because of the phone calls, early Sunday mornings, when Bill was still peacefully asleep. My hello, the long-distance *blip-bleep*, my mother-in-law asking abruptly for my husband. The privacy of their Spanish then, and later the translation truncated, for brevity's sake, into headlines: baby abductors found in the house next door; three months of *campesino* wages stolen in broad daylight; Bill's mother clobbered on the back of the head by an assailant; other assaults — at red lights, at stop signs, in the thick tourniquet of pollution around the bases of volcanoes. El Salvador had become a place in which merely remaining alive seemed an apparent coincidence, and we had stayed away for five ambivalent years until Bill's grandmother made her wishes known. *I will not die without my grandson.*

So Bill went home.

"Who are your best friends?" I once asked him.

"Periquito and Jaime and Chepe."

"But you never see them."

"It doesn't matter."

"You never write to them."

"It makes no difference."

"You don't even talk to them on the phone."

"Periquito and Jaime and Chepe will find me when they need me. That's all that matters with friends."

It was June, and Bill went home. Scented candles for his blind grandmother. Photographs of Jeremy for Bill's mother and aunts. Greetings from me that he would have to translate. Something elastic in his eyes.

"You're doing a good thing," I told him, my voice angry.

"It's my home. It's my grandmother. It's my friends."

"No driving on the back roads. No straying into alleys. No hanging around banks on payday."

"It's five days, Beth. Five. I'll be fine."

"It's El Salvador, Bill. El Salvador. That's the point."

But the point, in truth, was that Bill was finally returning home. He was going back to where it all begins — to the family he grew up with, to the memories that form his core, to the people who know his secret past and always, always will. Bill was going home, where a chair was waiting, and conversations, where it would be as it had been forever, despite so many years and so much distance. Some things inviolable. Some things impenetrable. Some friendships ever true, physiological, transcending.

Bill back home isn't Bill, he is William. To Periquito, who is also Lito, who is also Raphael, he is Chivago, a name, Bill says, that has no real translation but (because I keep pressing) might as well be interpreted as cool, round-about-town kind of guy. *But you hardly leave the house*, I say, propping my head up on the palm of one bent arm and doing a lousy job of suppressing my surprise. We are lying in bed, face to face. He is answering the questions I ask.

"Well, sure." He shrugs. "Sure. Here I don't."

"Because?"

"Because there's nothing to do."

"But back home...?"

"Back home there was always something to do, and the days and the nights were too short."

"How did you spend them?"

"What?"

"The days and the nights?"

"How else? I was a kid. I spent the days and the nights with my friends."

Here are the memories Bill gives me so that I can understand his childhood the way he does. First, imagine his neighborhood as it was thirty years ago: a row of upper-middle-class houses pinned to the very edge of civilization. Hectares of abandoned coffee farms form a natural theater just one block away—the shade trees huge and the coffee trees bony and gangs of kids from other neighborhoods always lurking, potentially, somewhere within. Beneath the houses (some brick, some stone, all of them gated and swarmed by pudgy flowers) lies an underground network of sewage and storm pipes, some big enough to walk through, some only eighteen slithery inches wide.

"I am the one with the imagination," Bill says, going back in time because I'm asking. "I decide what the plot is and which characters we need, and then we all go grab our little black cases and little fake telescopes and little plastic magnifying glasses and spend the whole day—or the whole week—solving the mystery."

"Who?"

"Periquito and Jaime and Chepe, and sometimes Jaime's cousin."

"Always the same cast of characters?"

"We were neighbors. Our mothers were friends. We were friends, too, which is what I'm explaining."

"Okay. I'm sorry. Keep going."

"Anyway, for obvious reasons, we inhabited the network of pipes. Dragged ourselves through on our bellies. I mean, we would go the length of entire blocks inside those pipes, getting our shoulders caught, they were that narrow. And getting filthy, of course. We were always filthy."

"What were you looking for?"

"Clues."

"What did you find?"

"Clues. And once, almost, a dead man. The newspapers reported his corpse the next day."

"A dead man?"

"Yes, a homeless guy, or a murdered guy. I'm not sure I ever knew. And once we found what we thought was a pond. Rocks on its bottom that we all dove for. Later we figured out that it was storm drainage, all the run-off muck from the streets. We stopped swimming there after a while."

"What else would you do?"

"Stuff. You know. Like, on the weekends, before dawn, we would all climb into the back of my grandfather's Jeep, and he

would take us up the mountain toward St. Anthony's. And as
soon as we'd reach the top of the mountain, we'd tumble out of
the Jeep and run back down the jungle cliffs toward the gorge.
We'd get to the river, and we'd wade in, waist high, and we'd
wander for hours in one direction or wander for hours in the
other. One morning all we did was watch a snake digest a frog.
And when we heard the horn of my grandfather's Jeep blasting,
we'd know that we had fifteen minutes, tops, to climb back up
the mountainside if we wanted Lenora's tortillas when they were
hot. And when my grandfather napped, in the afternoons, we
would climb the nearby fruit trees and eat what we picked. And
this is what Jeremy doesn't have, you know. This is the part of
life that he's missing."

"And when it rained?" I ask, not so deftly sidestepping the final comment. Bill knows that I know that we've circumvented
the boringness of our son's childhood. He lets me get away with
it this time.

"Periquito and I would bang a ball around in the garage, or
Chepe and I would get into fights."

"Fights?" I prod.

"Fights is what Chepe and I did. Which was sort of a joke after a while."

"And what else did you do—in general—what other things?"

"We would play soccer in the streets, throwing our tee shirts
down for goal posts. We'd light firecrackers on New Year's Eve.
We'd play marbles and spin tops and, well, we all lived nearby.
We were in and out of each other's houses, like brothers. We
wasted time, mainly. We had time to waste time, to be friends."

"So was it proximity, then?"

"What?"

"Proximity that started and sustained these best friendships?"

"That and the fact that we did what we did, and that family was involved, and that afterward we never forgot it. We never messed with the memories."

In going back home alone last June, Bill would finally be free — of translating, of explaining, of looking out for me. He spent every morning in the candle-scented dark by the bed of his relieved and failing grandmother. He spent the afternoons with Periquito, Jaime, and Chepe at the beach. I tried to picture them all while Jeremy and I waited here — a dentist, a manager, a salesman, my husband, now with not even a country in common. All I could see, in my mind's eye, was the gang of them flopped out — one thin, three portly, all four in squatty plastic chairs on those black, buggy, soggy sands, laughing contagiously at history. The thin guy reminding the three others of their youth. The three others looking to the thin guy for memories. This extension of friends into something like family. A continuum. A safe place. A rare and gorgeous relic.

"What do you talk about?" I would ask Bill at midnight when he called, everything about him so far away.

"We mostly remember," Bill would say. "It's all a ritual. We confirm that all those things really happened. In our minds, and out loud, we relive them."

"Isn't it hard to talk because you've been gone so long?"

"No. It's as easy as breathing."

"As breathing?"

"Yes. Easy as breathing. The conversation never ends."

In all of this, I think, Bill is like his mother, though years ago I would not have guessed that I'd have been satisfied with the resemblance.

My first meeting with Bill's mother was inauspicious; it set the pace. Only a month before our wedding, with Bill just a few days out of graduate school, I had transferred my belongings to the uppermost floor of that odd Camac Street rowhouse, a bold move that upped the rent a whole fifty dollars a month. Three guests were coming for a seven o'clock meal: my husband-to-be, his Salvadoran mother, and his mother's friend, a miniature white-haired thing whose name, Blanquita, was a divine inspiration. I had never cooked a formal meal before, and it was way too hot for June.

The evening's menu is seared into my mind. My first roasted chicken. My first baked potatoes. My first fresh green beans. Four sourdough rolls from the bakery two blocks south. A salad constructed from ordinary greens and lavished with store-bought dressing. Pepper, paprika, and salt were my handmaidens. I was relying on the paprika, especially, to give the meal a festive mien.

It was unseasonably warm, and to be certain that I'd avoid the gaffe of serving raw chicken, I slipped the bird and the potatoes into the oven around three in the afternoon. The apartment itself had been spotless for at least four days, and I was about to escape to the shower and prepare my own self for inspection when I heard the annoying beckoning of the buzzer. I rebuttoned my blouse and went flying down the steps—three flights' worth, now, of that awful bloody carpet, the staircase seeming that much narrower from the very top. I don't know who I was expecting, but not the foursome who stood at the door: Bill, his well-traveled mother, the little snowflake Blanquita, and Jane, a good-hearted friend of ours. Jane and the groom carried a trunk between them like a coffin. Bill's mother and Blanquita started up the steps in single file. I blinked and started leading them onward, wheeling heel after heel, tripping backward. *Hello, hello, hello,* I said. *And hello to you.* A hairy eyeball at Bill.

The third-floor apartment in that three-story rowhouse was drawn out like a question mark. There were no hallways, just three rooms that roughly swung in and out of each other. The furnishings were sparse: a futon, a mock kitchen table, four folding chairs, an easel, a desk. When the party reached the top of the steps, it teetered breathlessly for a moment, then made its way through the kitchen and into the back room, depositing the trunk beside the easel. It would have been nice, at that point, if there had been some comfy chairs for my overheated, out-of-breath, four-hours-early guests, but there were only the folding chairs at the kitchen table, making it every guest for himself or herself. Having already made her now-*she*-would-make-a-good-daughter-in-law impression, Jane begged off, claiming another appointment. When I closed the door behind her and returned to the back room, a swirl of Spanish conversation had started among my guests, who had plopped disconsolately on the floor. That, I believe, was the deciding moment. Had I been able to offer a snack—a few nice squares of cheese, some cracked-wheat crackers, some toothpicks (now *that* would have been the thing)—the visit might have gone swimmingly. But I had bought just enough for the seven o'clock meal, and water in tall glasses was all I could offer.

No matter. The guests began festooning the spare room with gifts. The trunk was either insidious or magical—it could hold at least four times more than its cubic physical limitations, and from its depths my soon-to-be mother-in-law began to pull pile upon pile of welcome-to-my-culture gifts. There were pots and pans and the family's antique sterling. Four silver coffee servers and all the attendant trays and spoons. Countless handmade linen runners, towels, and sheets. Enough terry cloth for the rest of my time here on earth. Enough sheets to host a small fraternity. The towels and sheets, it seems, were the gifts the two ladies were most proud of; speaking in Spanish to each other, they spread their wares before me on the glutted floor. My groom's last name begins with S, my first with B. In honor of yours truly, every towel, every washcloth, every pillowcase, every sheet was monogrammed BS in the largest letters I'd ever seen.

I knew even then that first impressions last a lifetime. I knew that my mother-in-law, on behalf of her eldest son, had trekked from Central America to bring me gifts. That Jane and Bill, in the afternoon heat, had lugged this huge trunk who knows how far between them, that Blanquita was gloating, and that everything on my floor had been laid there for my enrichment. I knew that I was already, in so many ways, a disappointment, and that my performance at this moment would prove key. But there were twenty-four twelve-inch BS's sprawled on my floor, and my eyes—I just couldn't help it—leaked like seaweed. I got a flash of my future, and it was one big BS. I would wake up with it and go to sleep with it. It was my destiny.

And that was just the prelude to dinner. By seven o'clock the chicken was, shall we say, done. The lemonade I had reserved for dinner had been swilled in late afternoon; we were down to water for refreshments. I hadn't taken a shower, I hadn't heard my own language for hours, I hadn't even stolen a kiss from my lover's lips, and the chicken was crusty, the beans overboiled, the salad—kindly put—plain. The best thing I had to offer that night was the rolls, served cold from the bag, with four alarmingly diminutive pats of butter. All through dinner I sat in the audience of Spanish, wondering, my teeth on edge, just what my guests were saying. It wasn't until many years later that Bill finally decoded the secret talk. *My mother was telling me to praise your cooking, no matter what comes out of the oven,* he confided. And come to think of it now, Bill—eternally faithful—always has done that.

I learned eventually to appreciate my husband's mother by watching her interactions with friends. By insisting that at least some part of her stories be translated. By saying: *Wait. You know some English. Tell me that story yourself.*

My mother-in-law, whom I call Nora, has traveled the world, but she's never really left home. Her friends today are the friends she grew up with—the children of her father's friends, the girls from her Catholic grammar school. Elba, Elsa, Flora, Mimi, Mima, not to mention her blood sisters, Adela, Marta, and Ana Ruth, who are part of the sweep of this family. White-haired now, and with an assortment of limps, the women travel together, daily share mugs of coffee, walk in a gang to morning Mass, arrive in an ensemble at funerals, share second homes and maids, pet monkeys, piñata trees, anything envied or wanted. Like grandchildren or diamonds. One by one through the years, through war, Nora's friends have lost their men to assassins, infidelity, accident, cancer, but they've gone on invincibly, their schoolgirl giggles following them everywhere, like an intoxicating mist. When they are not managing coffee in the hills or watermelon by the coast, when they're not running fancy clothes from Miami to their rich friends, when they're not in the orphanages, hospitals, nursing homes, or campaign headquarters, they're sitting around with their anecdotes, sounding like a flock of birds. Scratching the loose, weary skin on each other's brown arms. Knocking back bourbon. Remembering.

Nora today is not the woman in the scrapbook she gave Bill and me ten years ago. Then she had dark, luxuriant hair, she posed coquettish and sweet, her dresses cinched at the waist. Today the skin of her face pulls away from her eyes and billows down toward her chin; her lips are thin. Her waist has all but disappeared, and her hair, cropped short, is sparse. She wears loose-fitting dresses and a steel brace on one shoe, and still, at weddings and parties, she is a woman to be reckoned with, a woman who, with the slightest change in expression, can go from stately to severe and back to silly. She lost her second son to the chickenpox brought home by the maid's baby. She lost her father to a cancer that would not bow to drugs. She lost her husband the way too many women do, and she never had what she wanted most, a daughter. She's been robbed, beaten up, thrown from a horse; the white blossoms on her coffee trees have ripped away in storming weather. More than twenty years ago, Nora's sons started leaving home, and they're not coming back. She has a farm on her hands, she has her father's hard-won land, and the future of her country and of her farm remains uncertain. Nora's body carries all of this weight around. It becomes lighter when she's with friends, which is to say that it's leavened all the time, that she survives because of their tapestry.

I have been at the beach house, the surf pounding at the black crystalline sand, while Nora lies with her friends in the shade of old palm trees remembering scooter races on the cobblestone streets, remembering Los Chorros, where they flung themselves from rock cliffs into the far-down blue spring water. I have seen them line up at parties, these women in their tailored canary yellow, sunset orange, blue-green shifts, laughing uncontrollably about the trouble they made in third grade, the havoc they wreaked on the nuns. I have seen them go from London to Mexico to Sweden to the States, the official Salvadoran emissaries to their children's distant weddings, and I have seen them sitting with a pile of linens on their lap, sorting them for the bride. When one of them is sick, they all gang up on the sickness. When one is sad or broke, another changes the guest-room bedding and invites her in to stay. Their children are gone, and their husbands, too. They're getting old, but they will not be alone.

"What's the funniest thing your mother and her friends have ever done?" I recently asked Bill, and he debated with himself. The Miss Universe send-ups? The annual costumes? I wanted to know which costumes, so Bill told me: stuff they pull from their closets, their Catholic school uniforms, old party hats, sparkly debutante dresses. They start dressing up about noon and go on all day. It took me a moment to realize that Bill had present-tensed the story.

"They *still* do costumes?" I wondered.

"Annually," he said. "Without fail. They lock everyone out of the house except the maids, and they squeeze themselves into these clothes. Drink rum and pretend they're kids again. Then they take pictures for posterity."

I tried to imagine this—these swollen women in Catholic schoolgirl clothes, white-haired grandmothers in teenage evening wear, these moneyed baronesses giggling at pranks, rehearsing old crimes, walking around with their zippers undone, while the maids, their smiles tilted out of view, freshen the drinks and the salsa. I try to imagine friendships like these, which spit in the eye of all storms.

There are dozens, maybe hundreds, maybe thousands of people with whom we go shoulder to shoulder every day. In our communities, our schools, our churches, our jobs. The neighbor who lends the wheelbarrow and shears and then stands by to cheer on the tulips. The bookseller who sets aside the obscure title that he knows (because he knows us) our library is missing. The labmates at college, the deskmates at work, the Saturday afternoon bikers who glide between the cool, light purple shadows that we, and they, have come to love. People who live some part of their lives in parallel to some part of ours, whom we adopt as we move along. We adopt them, and we name them: colleague, companion, confidant, associate, sidekick, patron, confrere, even *friend.* We adopt them and celebrate them and claim they're part of us, and all of the sudden they're gone.

I want to know if there is anything riper or richer than the friendships of youth, which shape us twice, first in the present, then in the past. I want to know who will be here, for which rituals, when I'm sixty. What will I be reliving then? With whom will I remember?

Too many friendships barely outlive their contexts. Too many are merely serial, convenient, a way station, a passing through. We get jumbled together, we look sideways, we promise, and then the framework starts to crumble. Those whom we thought of as friends become strangers, so incidental that we barely remember, if indeed we do remember, how or why or even when they were part of us.

Bill, as I have mentioned, left Philadelphia just after I met

him, to pursue a master's degree in architecture. At his school he
found like-minded talents, and all that talent drew him in. With
a handful of others, he designed, debated, competed, learned; he
cast out the net of himself and hauled in friendships. For two in-
credible, passionate years, those friendships, those conversations, those competitions, were Bill's vapors. Those people were
the people in his life. And then, on a spectacular day at the end
of one May, the masters of architecture cleaned off their desks.
They wore black gowns and goofy hats and stringy ties around
their necks. They gathered in a garden and accepted awards for
Best This and Best That, stood there with diplomas in their
hands. They told the same tired jokes one last hysterical time,
then piled up together, arm over arm, on the concrete steps.
Cameras and humor and awe and relief jazzed and flashed and
fizzed. Then all those black robes got splattered with color—
with the yellow scarves, the ribboned blouses, the bright red
shoes of everyone else. Old lovers, old friends, long-lost parents,
sisters, brothers, pressed themselves in against the friends and
formed a crowd.

The result was a dilution, the end of an era: the context for
those friendships was gone. There was a flurry of weddings in
the years that followed, a weekend retreat, a few holiday cards.
But by the time the practice of architecture had become a colos-
sal disappointment, the lines between friends had all but vanished.

It's happened to me: I've been sucked in, pushed out,
drowned. I have worked for companies, imbibed their culture,
fallen dangerously deep into their thrall. Fallen into teams and
eager collaborations, into alliances and gossip and charged-up
talk, convincing myself that I was a revolutionary, that my many

sacrifices served an end. I've persuaded myself that the people on the job were more important than people elsewhere, and I've called that friendship and invested it with meaning, and I've neglected neighbors, family, my husband, my son, other friendships for this vital thing I had. And then, cataclysmically, I've found myself out of favor, out of a job, out on the street, used up, forgotten. The friends I thought I had didn't call me, didn't remember me at Christmas. They didn't even recognize me on the street after a while. Is it friendship, if it thrives only in containers? Is it friendship if, like fashion, it is bound to geography, ideology, popularity, mood?

Maggie wants to move to Colorado, to her college town and her college friends, and Beth, I am feeling deflated. It's my friend Lucy writing, from way across the country, in an intelligent, disembodied e-mail. *I want to tell her that it's wrong, that she just can't up and leave, that we've worked on us, that us is tangible, that us counts for just as much as those college friends. But is that what a friend would do, Beth — keep a friend from moving on? Is that how fragile I assume our friendship really is, that it won't survive a change in scene, a change in form?*

Friendship is a heat; we find its kindling everywhere. We find it in urgency and in pauses, we find it in the ripened tomatoes that our back-yard neighbors bring, in the predictable commentary at the local market. I find it when I sit with Anne in her sparse, ocher living room, talking about all things French, things delightfully foreign. And I say, *Now here's a friend. Here's a woman I can talk to. Here's a person I'll support, whose future I'll be a part of.* And then Anne, beautiful Anne, with her two chubby-cheeked, French-faced children, announces that it is time for them to go. Back to Paris where the apartments are too small, back to Paris and the crush of their old friends. Anne invites me, implores me, to schedule a visit, to promise a continuum, though we both admittedly ask: how likely is that? We have known each other as guests in across-the-street homes, and we do not know whether we will succeed in knowing each other by mail. We exchange gifts when we say goodbye. We exchange this prayer: that we will know each other always.

When you make a friend, do you assume that it's forever? Maybe, improbably, some of us do. I have suggested a calculus, a mathematics factored out of secrets told and entrusted, interests shared and expanded, debts assumed and repaid, masks removed and forgiven, needs expressed and simply answered — a methodology for lodging friends within our lives. But that's an inadequate math, for so many reasons. It's an equation that doesn't recognize what's true — that there are physical limits on the number of friends a soul can have — limits, especially, on best friendships. We cannot go on expanding our families ad infinitum. We cannot give, we cannot take, we cannot cherish in equal proportions, cannot perpetually widen our circles, giving equal weight to every friend. If we think we can — and I often think I can — we lose what we desired in the first place, we lose what makes us human, what makes us better than ourselves. We lose that intimacy, that clarity, that absolute assurance that our friend will be there when we need her, that we will be there for whoever dares ask for us. Aunt Carol, Aunt Loretta, Aunt Joan, and my mom. Elba, Elsa, Mima, Mimi, Flora, Nora, and Nora's sisters. Periquito, Jamie, Chepe, and Chivago. Friendship is a living thing. It needs room to grow.

8

She Was There
All Along

IT WAS JOANNE'S FATHER who nudged the first plank into place. A man of books and small details, he is more beautiful now that he is deep into his sixties, his tall, lean frame uncompromised by the years, his spectacular white hair resolutely going nowhere, his face as kind and as good as Geppetto's. He had seen my name in a local newspaper and mailed it to his daughter. She had done the remembering and the sleuthing that followed. And all this time—and here's the irony—Joanne's father and mother were living down the street, less than a mile from me. Right over there where I am pointing, beyond the hill and south, around the bend, in the cul-de-sac of gray townhouses. Every Friday a florist has brought them flowers, and every fourth or fifth or sixth Saturday or Sunday, Joanne and her family have driven up from their home, two hours south, to visit. They have brought more flowers. They have brought a grandson, they have brought a gorgeous new white-blonde granddaughter. They have stopped by throughout the cancers and the stroke that riddled Joanne's mother, through the bad news and the good, through the diminishings and perpetual uncertainty. All this time I thought Joanne had gone missing she's been here, visiting this very neighborhood.

Now we are making up for the twenty years we lost. Now we —Joanne, her husband, her children, her parents, I, my husband, my son, my parents—are getting to know one another for the first time and also again. Joanne and I are remembering the language we spoke, the comforts we used to give each other.

Tonight Joanne and her husband, Tom, will be our guests for dinner. It's not just the meal that preoccupies me now, or the house, or the appalling state of the silverware. While I soak and snip the spinach, while I damp-cloth the molding, while I sweep the front porch of bat droppings and leaves, I'm thinking about the talk we'll have. I have seen Joanne for short bursts of time since she found me and called me last fall. I have taken her back to my mother's house, driven with her on familiar roads, sat with her parents in that gray townhouse. I have said, *This is my husband*, and Joanne has said, *And this is mine;* I have said, *This is my child*, and she has said, *Meet Samantha and Michael*. I have said, *Remember this?* and she has answered, *Remember that? Remember him? Remember her? Remember us?* It's been surface stuff, a skimming and a sliding, in danger of skittering nowhere.

I know how much close friendships mean, and I know how much they cost. I know that if Joanne reenters my life, takes a seat at my family's table, tells me who she has become and what she thinks and what she sometimes needs, if she turns and wants the same from me, adjustments will be required, adjustments will be made. There will be more of us at the table, for one— more voices, more laughter, more pain. There will be more to attend to, more to stretch into, more and less of me than there was. There will be more magic, more worries, more peace, more strain.

Bill goes back home and finds his friends the same as when he left them. That's not the case for Joanne and me. We broke apart. We floated. We left things raw. There were regrets, apologies on both sides left unspoken. We have work to do, things that must be said, and as I wash the spinach, garnish the hens, smooth out the linens, I wonder: how much of myself can I yield, how well can I listen, how will I pry the lid off a jar shut and sealed twenty years ago? What is my talent for friendship, for reclaiming what I let slip away?

But then I think about what would happen if I turned my back on this bit of fortune, this unexpected rise in the wind. If I lost Joanne again, I would lose my history, our language, the secrets we shared. The way she laughs, the way she stands, the way she bends her hair around her ear. Twenty years ago I gave Joanne everything I was. She still has that. It's hers alone. She knows where I come from as no one else ever will. Joanne is my oldest friend. This is our second chance. We grow too old to lose old friends, and Joanne knows this as well.

Seven years ago, an urban Presbyterian church was widened with a window. Light, as Louis Kahn once said, is the measure of things already made, the giver of all presence, and so it was in this square, blighted church, where light came like a birthing, raw with color. The window was my mother's doing and devotion—her way of keeping her own mother alive and her brother, too, the one lost after a grueling battle with cancer, the other taken in the rupture of an instant, without warning.

My mother and I had shared the making of this window,

though it is more accurate to say that I had watched her set her mind on it and then watched her get to work. Together we had visited the cool, damp converted winery where stained glass windows were still made the old-fashioned way. We had sat among the craftsmen, the iconographer, the nun, the Egyptian lady who painted faces too small to be delineated by separate bits of glass. The place had a smell and a peaceable darkness, was strewn about with multihued cartoons, ten thousand square feet of handblown glass, a rumble of cutters, scissors, patterns, H-grooved channels of solder and lead. With the man in charge, we leaned over the shards and edges of my mother's window and talked about a ruby cross, two gentle sheep, a tree, a sky, blooms, four doves in flight, six sacred words: *Blessed are the pure in heart.* Once, near the end of this massive window's making, we were led up the steps to a room of sudden light, where my mother's stained glass remembrance, in near-complete ensemble, hung illuminated against the sun.

On the day of the window's dedication, family, friends, parishioners sat before my mother, with the realized window behind her. Sat in the pews of my mother's and my uncle's youth, where my grandmother herself had once sat. With the oratorical eloquence she continually proves that she has, my mother spoke of the two resting lambs and the four soaring doves, of the ephemeral and the everlasting. She spoke of what is given and of what is snatched away, and how light through a window carries memory.

My mother spoke of friends, the circle of ladies to which my grandmother belonged, to which she was tied, in life, in death. At the pulpit, my mother named the ladies, a generation gone, and then she put my grandmother at the center of the circle. My brother, sister, and I had known my grandmother as musk-smelling and brave, a woman with silky bright dresses, flamboyant hats, gloves closed at her wrists with two faux pearls. A legendary good luck charm, she famously won at the races, and once she brought home an ugly painting and, on a hunch, ripped apart its backing papers to find a hoard of dollars. She lived behind the bright green door in a neighborhood of black doors. There was a spot on the rug where she'd danced the jitterbug. There were marks on the kitchen wall where, laughing, she'd thrown her homemade cakes—failed experiments all—to see if they would bounce. In my grandmother's cellar were her trunks and hangers full of clothes, faded cardboard album covers, my uncle's report cards, my mother's autograph books, my grandfather's roll-top desk, all part of her, part of the lady who came to our house at Easter with baskets full of strings and clues, with gifts we'd have to find. As a child, I loved my grandmother with such utter fierceness that for years following her death I was sure that every cloud contained her whisper.

But that day in southwest Philadelphia, my mother introduced a Margaret Finley D'Imperio I had never known. She turned back the clock and made her young, put all these women in her company, and conjured the sounds of her many lasting friendships. I had a hard time thinking that my grandmother had been shared in such a global fashion, that so many others had been the beneficiaries of her time, her passions, the laugh behind her hand—had had the pleasure of this Irish woman's meatballs, this good horse-betting Presbyterian's charms.

Those women taught one another hymns, my mother said that day, and sang them in one another's kitchens. And when it got too hot in my grandmother's long, thin, tight brick rowhouse, they sat out on her stoop overlooking the playground and planned showers and birthday parties, charity work, Wildwood days. They passed around recipes for gravy.

These were my grandmother's friends. They were her neighborhood, her church, her roots, her family, her one nation, under God, indivisible. Being with them, doing with them, talking with them, singing with them was part of who she was. My grandmother grew old with these friends, and surely there were times—as surely as there were those friendships—when a lie was told or a joke offended or somebody dropped her skein of thread, only to have it picked up again by someone else, who understood that the endurance of the friendship mattered more than the infraction.

How does a tree take all the weather in its stride? How does it fatten the wood around its pith despite windstorms, drought, insects, and flood? I have lived a restless life. I have expanded and retracted. I have been angry, I have trusted. I have been a student, a loner, a wife, a colleague, a neighbor, and a friend, and I have also been the opposite, dismissing failed relationships for the glimmer of new ones, pulling the plug on my own history, assuming that somewhere someone else would fill the very particular void that only one person can fill.

But friendship involves more than that. It involves—it absolutely requires—persuasive acts of mercy. I suspect that my grandmother and her crowd had so many lifelong friends because they understood the word *essential.* They understood roots, trees, the seasons; they were not afraid of their own shadows. I'd like to have the courage they had. I'd like Joanne to be here when I'm sixty. I would like my son to bear witness.

. . .

Thinking of tonight, I run conjured conversations through my mind like operettas. I think of the questions I might ask Joanne, the things I want to know, the risks I'm willing to take for the sake of laying down more planks. I craft strategies for pulling our husbands into the talk and also strategies for closing them out—divergent conversational paths for them to follow while Joanne and I get to the real business of us. I smile, thinking of the people we'll remember, the jokes no one will get but us. I consider unveiling all the plans I have, the things I dream of doing. I imagine her telling me about her life in Maryland, about her summers on the beach, about the courses she is taking, how she is growing, at long last, into her faith. *Do you remember when Dr. Dewsnap let me play Juliet to Jim's Romeo?* I'll ask her. *Do you remember that Halloween we dressed like a train and couldn't turn the corner in the stairwell? Do you remember Annie? Well, I saw her the other day. She was wearing a hat and her eyes were bright green and I remembered, all of the sudden, how her brother passed away.* Any scripted conversation is bound to be a farce, but if, academically, I know this, it doesn't stop my mind from rambling.

Here is what I've been doing all day with my hands while my head has gone off concocting. I have layered the washed spinach with sautéed mushrooms and scallions in a broad baking pan, sprinkled it all with grated cheese, sealed it with cellophane, put it aside. I have done the hens up like some kind of Yuletide offering—garnishing them with green, red, golden flavors. I have laced lettuce with raspberries, found a basket for the bread, done my best with the rosy new potatoes, prepared a fresh plate of butter. I have circled the house thrice, hunting down dust mice, tidying up *Newsweeks*, hiding my *People* magazines, polluting the air with the stench of bleach, lemon, ammonia, stain busters, the unnaturally downy smell of Tide. I have set the table and stacked it with candles, and I have opened the door to find my mother standing there, a smile extended, a pot of miniature roses in her hands. *Give my best to Joanne, will you, Beth? Tell her that I too have missed her.*

And when the meal is finally tamed and the house is as good as clean and I have kissed my mother on the cheek, I have gone into the living room to do nothing. To sit on this long black couch—among shadow puppets and a lighted turtle, among Salvadoran statuettes and shards of old clay, among drawings made by my husband and my son—in the spare quiescent moments before Jeremy comes home from school. *What do you think about when no one's looking?* I'll ask Joanne. *When did your mother grow into someone so brave? When did your father become the elegant creature he is, or was he always like that, is it I who has changed, so that I can see him for what he is? And what roots you to this earth, Joanne? And how often do you marvel at the sky?*

I close my eyes and throw my head back against the couch leather, releasing its animal smell. To freeze my circuitous thoughts I listen for silence until it seeps through like a welcome wind. Calm, I open my eyes again, and I am confused at first by what they find. Looking down from the ceiling in the middle of winter, going nowhere, is Joanne's ladybug. A scarab of red with a sprinkling of black freckles. A single ladybug hanging up there, catching the light through the window.

Every ladybug is me, every ladybug is proof that I am still, somehow, alive. Isn't that what Joanne's mother-in-law had said on her very last day of life? Isn't that the tale Joanne, just weeks ago, had passed on faithfully to me? This is the rest of my old best friend's true story: *The ladybugs found me. They did. Not just at the funeral, but afterward, on Samantha's hair, on windowsills, in other people's houses, the ladybugs came.* All of a sudden I feel that something bigger than myself is here with me in this excessively clean house. I get the sense, stronger than instinct, that this ladybug is both messenger and message. Crazy with the notion that I can somehow keep it in view, I talk to it for a little while, tell it hello, I've heard its story. I think of my grandmother with all her charmed luck, her tight circle of friends, the clouds that might still hold their whispers.

Perhaps it's true, as James Boswell wrote, that we cannot tell the precise moment when friendship is formed, or reformed. That drop follows drop into an invisible vessel until something important and crucial overflows. But maybe it is equally true that friendship demands a stunning leap of faith. That no question, no answer, no amount of dialogue will matter so much as the inexplicable ties that bind one to another: the cakes that bounce, the horses that win, the Italian meatballs in an Irish woman's pot, the suspended friendship that hovers for years until courage, good fortune, pulls it back down to earth. There's a ladybug on my ceiling in the middle of winter, and my old best friend is coming for dinner. That's enough for now. That's enough for a while. I go to the phone to let her know that someone's here with me; we both are waiting.

9

Top of the World

"IF SOMEONE CALLED YOU STINKY, I would tell them you were not," James declares out of the blue on a prematurely warm day.

"Yeah," Jeremy nods zealously. "That's right."

"Because you're not stinky." James solidifies his position. "You're definitely not."

Jeremy nods again, supremely satisfied by James's assertion in the face of this imagined scenario.

"You're not stinky and nobody gonna say that you are," James promises. "Nobody, when I'm around, calls you stinky."

"Why all the talk about stinkiness?" I ask James. The subject has arisen over a stalled game of Mouse Trap. The boys have gotten no further than reading the instructions in Spanish, which is funnier than the game could ever be.

James explains that it has to do with recess. A classmate, a boy, was being taunted. "They were calling him stinky and I smelled him and he's not," James explains, with a harrumph of his chin to make the point. "So I ran to the teacher and I told her big time, and she blew her whistle and made it stop."

"Jeremy," I say, the wise response predictably fugitive, "aren't we lucky to know James? To know someone as strong as he is, and as brave?"

Jeremy throws the feather of his arm across the continent of James's shoulders. "Yup," he says, beaming. "Yup, we are. James is our friend."

"I think that makes you a hero, James," I say, but James will have none of this. He flexes his astonishingly versatile face into a knobbed nose and a canyoned mouth, until all I can see is his tongue. "Nah," he says. "The kid didn't stink. You can't call a kid stinky if he's not."

Later the boys retreat to the air, the yard, a game of hide-and-seek. They rush to tree stumps and deck chairs, to the maples on the periphery, James wearing dragon-fire red, Jeremy dressed in a shirt as bright yellow as the new Volkswagen bugs. No amount of ducking, nipping, gymnastics will shrink them from view. Still, each pretends to be blind to the other's bright colors. They pretend not to hear the ruckus that spurts out from the nook in the climber, the giggle from behind the wheel of the car, the snigger from the old love seat on the deck, its black and white fabric stripes now faded to a monochromatic gray. I think about the kids on the playgrounds around here. I think about Jeremy and James and how exceptional these two are, how impeccably reverential of each other's pleasures. James lets Jeremy believe he's still hidden. In a few minutes the favor is returned. *Where are you? Where are you?* one calls to the other in my jejune and unmysterious back yard. *I'm right here,* comes the answer, the confession. Still the seeker troops on by, buying the hider his moment of glory.

Watching them through the cobwebbed window, I feel suddenly sad: life is too ephemeral. I grab a camera, and through the spider's veil I take photographs of the boys running, spoofing, laughing, allowing each other to win. I gather evidence of their goodness, proof of a bond that I cannot, in any enduring way, keep whole. This friendship is James's and Jeremy's. Its future lies in their hearts.

Time passes. I leave the window that looks out on the boys and sit on the caved-in swivel chair. I think about the boy James saved from stinkiness, and what that means, in the scheme of things, about friendship. It takes work, James is learning. It doesn't come for free. Friendship has rules that must be played by.

An etiquette defines every successful friendship, unspoken at times, but always there. Even the most casual society is knit together by tacit understandings about what is and is not done among members. According to Hemingway in *A Moveable Feast*, at the Closerie des Lilas, one of the best cafés in Paris, "Most of the clients were elderly bearded men in well worn clothes who came with their wives or mistresses and wore or did not wear thin red Legion of Honor ribbons in their lapels.... These people made it a comfortable café since they were all interested in each other and in their drinks or coffees, or infusions, and in the papers and periodicals which were fastened to rods, and no one was on exhibition."

A boy in a schoolyard is called stinky. James, his friend, defends the boy's honor. It's just one responsibility among many. As James and Jeremy grow older, there will also be the responsibility to listen, to anticipate, to remember, to share, to forgive, to overlook, to just plain be there. There will be gifts to give and to receive, tediums as well as horrors to witness and relieve.

Even in the most debasing circumstances—the concentration camps of the Holocaust, say—you find friends honoring friends, taking care. "It was astonishing to see how anxious these hungry men were to share what they had," one man remembers in Terrence Des Pres's *The Survivor.* "There was half an orange on all the beds in the room. One of our friends had received a parcel. He had not even been able to wait for our return." Another survivor recalls that Ilse, who worked on the day shift, returned at noon: "She turned away from me so that I could not see what she was doing, and dug into her pocket. 'I brought you a present,' she announced triumphantly. There, on a fresh leaf, was one red, slightly mashed raspberry."

I expect certain things from each of my friends, and they each hold expectations of me. This is friendship's justice. When I have been frightened by an illness that will not go away, by the bullet of a migraine or the endurance of bronchitis, I call Ellen, my doctor friend, with a list of symptoms, a set of fears; she answers, appeases, tells me what to do next. When I have been angry, Tom has listened and put the facts in perspective; he's helped me see what is real, what is not. I have had many birthdays, and Jamie has remembered each one. I have been frustrated with the kids I teach, worried about the son I raise, filled up with news I want to share, and Vicki, in quiet moments at the school, listens, and Lori calls and reassures and helps me get out of myself. I have hated my writing, and Susan has brought me peace. I have waited in the school lobby for word of my son's performance in a third-grade spelling bee, and Kathy, Jeremy's teacher (who is also now my friend), has hurried—*hurried*—to find me, hugged me as she's told the news, let the tears fall as she says, *You would have been so proud, Beth. I was so proud myself.* And in all of this there's reciprocity. I listen decorously to Ellen's disappointments, help Tom weigh questions, bring Jamie flowers, think through issues with Vicki, laugh at nothing with Lori, carefully critique Susan's smart short stories, buy Kathy the most gorgeous piece of Venetian handblown glass that the stores have to offer. That is the privilege and the equation. We take care of the people we love. We go back and forth, giving of ourselves to those we have chosen for our lives. And sometimes our lives seem impossibly full, and instinctively we shut the door on could-be, would-be friendships.

No friendship, I'm realizing, survives without the passionate exchange of stories. Without each one carrying the other along for the rides we've independently taken. I've lately started to understand how deep a friendship might go, how long it might last, how much I *want* it, by the care with which the stories are told. By the time someone takes with what I say and how much time I want to give to what they have to tell me. The balance is not always easy to come by; I may tell a new acquaintance my stories only to discover that he does not intend to tell many of his own. I reveal, he doesn't. I write letters, he sends postcards. I hurt, and he barely acknowledges that hurt, I send gifts, and he hardly mentions their arrival—all the while carrying on the pretense of friendship. The relationship won't last. We don't mean the same things to each other.

Right now, so many of the stories that stretch my soul come to me through the ether. Doug, Susan, Eliot, Kate, Eric, Judy, Adam, Amy, Nancy, Lucy, Ken, Linda, Jean, Tom, Aubrey— each writing their stories to me, and I writing my stories back in a swale of language, lost punctuation, the clever brevities of electronic mail. My archives are full of frozen bits of talk and consolation, encouragement and advice, reviews of books, scenes from a train, scenes from a hospital, scenes from a marriage, scenes through windows at night. A neighbor's peony. A dislocation. A dissatisfaction. A job. Kate's Christmas tree— alive, carnal, quavering, liberating: *There's a refrigerator full of eggs and cheese and apple cider and thin red candles in the dining room for the little Christmas carousel we got when Zachary was four. Our tree expired dramatically the night we got it last week, but it looks pretty from across the room (though if you touch it the needles pop off to that tinkling Vince Garaldi music from "Charlie Brown"). Camille and I let the kids open the presents they got for each other while we sank into the couch with our eggnog in utter disbelief that we now have — what? — twelve days to do nothing but family. Epiphany indeed!*

For the longest time my world at large was a neighbor's handwritten notes stuffed in my mailbox. Things have changed, but still, I lead a very quiet life, a life primarily of hushed reflection. Now it is to this box on my broken trestle desk that I often turn to vicariously slip out on adventure, to that cruise ship in the warm waters where Doug is sailing, or into the classroom where Sandy is teaching, or out on the stoop where Lucy sits minding her kids, a block party in progress. It's where I go to find Judy remembering, where she lets me into her life: *I could hear the crickets on a summer night in Virginia, breezes in the woods out back, which we called the Bamboo Forest, and I could smell autumn coming, and hear the cheers from the football game at the public high school in our back yard. How I yearned to be part of that scene. And I could taste the strawberry rhubarb pie that only my grandmother could make, and that we ate on our visits to her North Dakota farm.*

My friends' tales are where I go when the boys are playing make-believe outside or when my husband and son are asleep, and someone is out there, restless. Their stories change the quality of the silence in the house when Jeremy's at school and Bill's at his job, when my neighbors are gone, doing whatever takes them from their houses. Their stories are the way a few rare people keep me posted on their lives—on Nancy's move to a new job in the south; on Aubrey's passions—she's taken up the cello; on Charlotte, who has fallen ill and has moved from the thrifts to intensive care: *Right before the surgery,* Amy writes, *she took out her teeth, and that's when I remembered that she really is a very old woman.*

Once I wanted only the kind of letters that the mailman or a neighbor brings, the bleeding handwriting on scratchy paper, the lines through words, the subtle reverses, the evidence of a thought in progress. For a long, long time I resisted cyberspace, scoffed at the pretense of reaching out to what could not be seen, touched, heard—to faces, in some cases, that couldn't be conjured. But I've grown to hunger for the word play, the images that bob behind the glass, for the assurance they give me that at least right now, today, I've been remembered, by someone far away. People are floating in the dark space just beyond my reach, and they have stories to tell. *Yesterday we took the train to buy Sky a bicycle,* Ken writes, yielding a mood of instant pleasure. *I spent most of the day running beside her, my hands on her back.*

I live on a street inhabited by taxi drivers and mill widows, Susan tells me. *The woman next door to me has buried two husbands and a child. A retired librarian, she's become an armchair genealogist, of course, and her computer's hard drive is filled with her family history. She's a blessing of a neighbor. She leaves tomatoes and cucumbers on my picnic table and watches over our house when we go on vacation. Though one day last spring she said, "I just got the most beautiful gift this morning. When I looked through your dining room window, I could see right into your master bedroom. The pink camellia outside your bedroom window was blooming, framed by the blue bedroom wall-paper. It was just like a picture. Can you see me while I'm working on my computer at my desk?" I hadn't. But this neighbor had looked all the way through my house, and I wondered what else she had seen.*

I wondered too. I wondered about the southern town where Susan lives, about the vegetables arranged on her picnic table, the camellia, the wallpaper, the cab drivers and mill widows, none of which I've ever seen. And I wondered about Susan herself, whom I briefly met years ago. When I close my eyes and think very hard, her likeness comes back to me, but only vaguely. And yet Susan is here always, in the gentle parabola of her magnificent stories, the weaving she does of my life with hers. I can't touch it. I can't see it. I can't hear it. I can't feel it. But her lovely, lyrical, languaged soul is right there, as the others are, on the opposite side of this glass.

The afternoon fades. I hear the front door bang open. Jeremy is prancing, James is clopping down the hall. The whites in James's eyes stand out as bright as two stars above the galaxy of his more-than-white smile. "Come be our audience," they say to me breathlessly, as tangible and true as any moment. "Where are we going?" I ask, a formality, for I know this part of the routine. I rise from where I've been sitting, leave the computer humming. James and Jeremy and I turn the quick corner into the living room, a room that, despite the smallness of our house, is seldom entered. I take my place on the black leather couch. The boys busy themselves in the corner.

Encircling us is the physical stuff of my life: the endangered beetles, the seashells, the exotica, the masks I've smuggled from lands I've traveled to and loved. A bull's skull from an abandoned apple warehouse in Santa Fe, clay dolls from a sliver of a storefront in Seville, miniature crystals from a street in Prague, where the clock sung and the brides danced and overgrown puppets wagged and perversely waddled—a street where friendship was given to me by a real, true writer, a talent and a heart, who has stayed in touch since. This room is the museum of me, the affidavit of my existence, witness to my having come, having gone. This room is mine, save for that corner over there. It is all but silent except when James is here. Right now he's letting the juice into the wires.

Here comes the show. Jeremy stands above the electronic keyboard. James has the karaoke mike pressed to his lips. We get "Crocodile Rock" first, with a dance/funk rhythm. Then we get "Killing Me Softly," pegged to a jazz/fusion beat. The volume goes up under Jeremy's direction, but not loud enough to drown out James, who was born to sing, born to dance, born with a microphone in his hand. James is all Baptist gospel talent, and when he doesn't know the words, he makes them up, fabulous non sequiturs that cripple Jeremy with a gigantic guffaw, a bellyache. Tears of laughter splash down Jeremy's face. It's not a trickle; it's water through a hose. The keyboard itself is getting wet, and now it's Jeremy's turn to sing and James's turn to man the keyboard, and separately they collect themselves, sniffle themselves straight. Now we get Mendelssohn's "Wedding March," "The Entertainer," "Happy Birthday," "Danny Boy," and "Greensleeves," in that all-nonsense order. Jeremy spends most of his mike time wiggling, not singing, while James, his profound hands on the pristine keyboard, urges him on. Between songs James makes grave and important announcements about Coke from the bar and the upcoming tour and the fans, whose autographs he promises to sign. I clap, I praise, I'm a whole roomful of people, I'm everyone I ever knew. I tell them the bull and the beetles are impressed. I tell them I hear their spirits clapping. I think about how friendship needs this, too: jumping into the unplanned, even the silly.

"I got an idea," James says all of a sudden, cutting the music.

"Yeah?" Jeremy says. "What is that?" James presses his lips to Jeremy's ear, and Jeremy smiles, shuffles over to me, takes my hand, asks me to stand.

"What's this, audience participation night?" I ask. But I don't get an answer. "What am I, the new emcee?"

But I don't get an answer, and now James is again busy at the keyboard, running his finger across the list of one hundred programmed songs until he finds the tune of his dreams. It's the Carpenters' "The Top of the World," a song I vaguely adored when I was young.

"This one's for you," James tells me. "It's an oldy but goody for you."

"Why thank you, boys," I say, sniffing, feigning injured feelings. "An oldy but goody, indeed. What am I, your grandmother?"

"I don't know the words," James says. "So you gotta teach me. Teach us both. You gotta teach us the words."

"The words?" I say. I suddenly feel a little shy. I remember Karen Carpenter's personal tragedy better than I remember her lyrics. But there's no time for shyness when you're in the company of friends, when a circle is being widened, or a moment. There's no time to step away from the story you are writing together. "Such a feeling's coming over me," I start out tentatively, my nose crinkled, my mind spazzing toward memory. "There is something-something in everything I see."

"Something-something?" James declares in disappointment. He cuts the music. "Something-something? What's something-something?"

Jeremy falls down laughing. "Yeah. Well," I go on, undeterred, pulling Jeremy up from his knees. "Yeah, well, I'm not as old as you think." James restarts the music, I go on: "Not a cloud in the sky, got the sun in my eye, and I" (and here I stomp my foot to emphasize the beat) "wouldn't be surprised if it's a dream." I sing the same verse two or three times because I don't know the first thing about the rest. I try out my voice. Yes. It works.

"Okay." James claps when he realizes I've hit my mother lode of memory. "Okay, that's good." He turns the music off and starts it over again, and then he goes cheek to cheek with Jeremy, lips to the mike, everything physical here, nothing separating them, no glass. James and Jeremy grab me by either hand, and all of us are singing now, Jeremy and James smudging their voices over mine, all three of us shouting *something-something* when we hit a bump. We get to the chorus: "I'm on the top of the world, Looking," *stomp* "down on creation, and the only something-something I can find..." We're singing so loud that our neighbors can hear us. We're singing so loud for the moment. We're singing so loud, and that's the story I'll later tell my friends in the dark, when my house is asleep, my words tapping lightly against their window glass.

10

A Sudden
Turn of Events

IT IS ODD TO BE BACK in the old neighborhood, straddling a
wooden chair in Andrée's cluttered kitchen. The one-way
streets in this part of town have been reversed, and I almost
got lost on the way. After I found a place to park, I wrapped a
scarf around my head and walked the sidewalk in a hurry.
Afraid of being recognized. Afraid of being forgotten. Febru-
ary, and impossible to tell whether things are prettier here or
worse.

A little girl, Andrée's youngest, answered the door when I
knocked. She wasn't more than a bulge in her mother's body
when I moved away five years ago, and that means I hardly know
her, and of course she doesn't know me. Andrée, too, seems unfamiliar. She is pale, her expression caught somewhere between
shock, denial, anger, and prayer. Her hair falls to the line of her
chin, then bluntly stops short. She blows on her glasses, rubs
them clean, returns them to her nose, looks hard and helplessly
at me. "Have some orange juice," she insists, and pours a glass
for me. When I leave it untouched, she hefts a bag of clementines in a straining plastic net to the table — an offering of sorts.

I keep looking at Andrée, keep snatching glimpses out her window past the dual asphalt strips and the mess of molting weeds. The house I used to live in is still defiantly turquoise, yellow, red. The lace curtains I once hung in the dining room are there still, steeped to the color of tea by long exposure to the sun. The house has a midday, midwinter darkness: no lights are on. It doesn't belong to me anymore. Maybe it never really did.

In Andrée's house everything is awkward. I have rushed here with roses, with books, with genuine concern, but what is there to say? *I am so sorry.* What is there to do? *Make the bad thing go away.* Why have I come? I wonder, sitting here. I wonder whether Andrée needs me, or whether I simply need to believe that she does. I question myself, but I know the truth. I am here because of our friendship. Because friends help friends face what can't be faced.

I get up. Pace a patch of her linoleum floor. Attempt to joke with the little girl who has come to the kitchen asking for milk, asking for help with her Barbie, asking her mother to read her a story right now, this instant. To the child I am an inconvenience. I glance out the window again and back around the kitchen, my eyes catching on a collage of photos clipped to the refrigerator door. There is a man, there are children, there is a woman whose lush, dark, magnificent hair sweeps to such a length that it seems, at least from my viewing distance, that it never ends. I move a step or two closer and bend in toward the collage. Yes. The long hair never ends.

"Andrée?" I ask, startled. "Is that you?"

"It was," she says. "Once."

"And him," I say. "That's him?"

"Yes. The two of us. Together."

"And those are the kids?" I ask. H and J. Before I ever knew them.

"That was a long time ago," Andrée says. "I don't know." She fumbles, gets up. "I just thought it might help to pin the memories where I could see them."

"You have to tell him," I say. "You have to go to him and tell him. About the pictures you found. The memories."

"Do you want lunch?" Andrée asks. "Aren't you hungry?"

The roses have been stuffed into a vase of water, their stems torn open to the taste of sugar. We have already run out of things to say, and the afternoon is young. I am here to bear witness. To throw myself between her and the thing I cannot possibly stop. I am here as her friend, and it's painful.

Who among us dares imagine last things: last word, last thought, last diffusion of light, last, last, final kiss, last sound? Who doesn't think, in a bold, brave, private place, that they will outsmart their destiny, outwit the risks, ooze themselves toward eternity? Death, after all, is not the only fate. Consider the sponge, as deathless as they come. Or a virus, crystallized for thousands of years like stone, which will, with a brush of dew, bloom back to life. Bacteria, for their part, bow to the religion of division — the parent not passing away but passing on, into its offspring, all those fractions of itself forever.

I believe in forever, don't you have to? Isn't that the only thing you or I can conceive of? *Andrée. I promise you. He'll live.*

But what are the odds? What are the chances? Two weeks the doctors have given her husband, maybe a month. "It was just a cough," Andrée says. "An inconsequential wheeze. He was on vacation, visiting family. He had a ticket to come home." She is beyond crying, at least for today. She is trying to picture the prayer house near Seoul where her husband has gone to fast and to have a talk with God. "How does he sound?" I ask. "Calm," she says. "Brave. And very far away."

"Mommy, I'm hungry," the little girl complains. "I'm hungry and I want to watch a movie, and I want to go outside and play."

"Let me take you to lunch," I tell Andrée. "Both of you. You choose the place."

"Right," she says.

"Where should we go?"

"I don't know," she says. "Let me think."

In silence, then, we sit until I, conjuring the prayer house, say, "But he was always far away."

"Right. He always was. He was like a whole separate country in my life."

It isn't too late. I want to reach across and hug her, tell her, *It isn't too late. It will be all right, I promise.* But I am impotent sitting here. I can't fix this, and I haven't yet brought comfort. I get up and look at the photos again. "You were beautiful," I tell her. Behind me she shrugs. "And look at him," I insist, as if bringing her into a garden of blooms. "He was proud you were his wife."

"Right," she says.

"No," I say. "Really. Look." And I pray to God that she sees what I see in the expression on his long-ago face. I pray that I can help her see. That I can honor her, friend to friend, that my presence here will somehow strengthen her for what's yet to come.

We married foreigners, Andrée and I. She a South Korean man, I a Salvadoran. When we were neighbors years ago, we shared a lot of things—not merely a fence and weeds and a bark-shedding tree, not merely poems and stories, encouragement, but the sense we sometimes had of being outsiders in our respective marriages. When I'd say my mother-in-law was coming to town, few understood as Andrée did. When I'd say that Nora's boisterous Salvadoran friends were coming too, and maybe even her sisters, Andrée would nod knowingly. I'd describe how the house would fill with the sounds of Spanish, how the noise of it rendered me both deaf and apoplectic, and how I would hear my name in the swirl—*Beth, Beth*, amid pointed fingers—and never really know what the *Beth* attached to, whether the things being said were kind or subversive. I wished fiercely that I was pretty so that I could sit within the clamor, indignant. Or that I was a bird with wings. Or that I knew Spanish.

Andrée understood when I told her these things. She had her own wealth of experience.

But Andrée tried harder than I did. She attempted assimilation right from the start, marrying her husband on a hill in South Korea. She told me once how overwhelming it was. *They were all black-haired women*, she said, *and they painted me up like a bride, talking the whole time amongst themselves, leaving me, in my white dress, in the dark.* They teased her hair into a crown, she said. She sealed her fate with a *neh*. They carted in a cake for a photo opportunity, then carted it to another wedding on the opposite side of the hill. *I always wondered*, she would sometimes say, *who got to eat that cake.*

Andrée was a good Caucasian wife to a strictly South Korean man. She learned how to cook the meals her husband liked, how to find the ingredients in ethnic shops on the fringes of the city. She learned how to entertain, how to build her house around the customs of Korea. No shoes past the front porch. No limits on the number of visitors. No demand that conversation be translated for her. No end to her hospitality. And in what was surely a testament to her wifely loyalty, she edited the theses of her husband's doctorate-seeking friends for free. No easy job, that, for these were would-be Korean ministers muddling through arcane scraps of holy history, Ph.D. candidates writing in a language they could hardly speak. It was absurd, but Andrée found humor in the chore. *Picture a page of print,* she would tell me. *Picture being left alone, without a compass, in the thicket of Apocalypse history with names like Kwang Suk Suh and Kidok Shinbo and Pasoo Koon. You feel betrayed by dependent clauses that lead you along through a string of commas and then right up against the brick wall of a period. And that's just the opening paragraph, on page one. That's just the start of a three-hundred-page tome.* Andrée, nevertheless, persevered, and in doing so paved the way for at least a half dozen Ph.D.s.

But none of that lessened the distance between Andrée and the man she married. There were terribly difficult, confounding times punctuated by small grace notes of calm. There were always so many questions. Having lived this long in a bicultural marriage, I have come to believe that perhaps the best we can do is to give each other room. To appreciate the strangerliness of one's lover as one does the treasures in a museum. To recognize that his foreignness is not what he does to you, but what he retains for himself, and that you, in the end, are a foreigner, too, corralled by the idiosyncrasies of your own geography and blood.

Sitting with Andrée now, I imagine that she is thinking, mostly, about distance. About the fifteen hours of sky between herself and her husband, about the years that have tripped and stumbled by since her wedding cake departed. He has been to Seoul dozens of times since he heard his wife say *neh*. She has never once found her way back there—too much an outsider, she would say, and far too busy with the children, four in all, who may or may not understand what is happening now. Andrée herself doesn't understand. How could she? How could anyone? He had gone to Seoul for a birthday party. It was just a cough; he got a checkup. Now the doctors are predicting that he'll never make it home.

Tell me what to say to Andrée. How to fix her broken heart. Give me the power to change her future. Give me a prayer God will hear.

"Mommy, I'm hungry. Please, Mommy, I am." The little girl plants her elbows on either side of the clementines and gets us to see her through our silence. She is the spitting image of him and also the spitting image of her, a virtual replica of her older brothers and sister. A few weeks ago, when life was on an even, casual keel, Andrée mentioned in a letter that this daughter had become her dearest friend. *She gets my jokes*, Andrée had written, and for me, that said it all. I'd felt comforted, reading that letter twice, that Andrée now had her soulmate. I'd felt also that her married life was calm, that husband and wife, now middle-aged, were finally growing more alike than they had been foreign. I had the illusion that Andrée was safe, that she finally had what she deserved, and a part of me had stopped worrying about a part of her. Don't take a single day for granted. Don't take an hour. Don't take a husband, or a wife. Please God, don't let the dying man die in the prayer house on the hill.

"We'll go to the Greek place," Andrée says. "It's just down the road."

"Fine," I say. "Good." I stand and straighten my slacks.

"But I want cereal," the little girl says. "Please, Mommy? Cereal?"

"We'll find something you like at the restaurant," I tell the child. "I promise." My attempt at sweetness sounds like what it is, an attempt.

"But I want cereal," she pouts, and then, when she discerns that the intruder's mind is made up, she skips off to get her coat and to summon up a Beanie Baby. Andrée goes off to get something, too. I'm alone in the kitchen with the photos. A Fourth of July parade, the first son in diapers held up to see. A family outing on a garden lawn. The wife in a peasant blouse, her shoulders draped with all that hair. The husband propped against a long brick wall, his posture betraying nothing of his future. Time passes. Andrée returns. I hear her step up behind me.

"You're going to Korea," I tell her. "You're going to get on a plane and go."

"He's in a prayer house," she says. "Fasting. Meditating. Working on his *qi*. They don't make room there for the healthy."

"I don't care," I insist. "You're going. You're his wife. For you they have to change the rules."

"They don't know me from Adam in Korea," she protests, "and besides, I've got all these kids, and I have a lousy bedside manner, and I'm clumsy, you know? And I don't know what I'd say, I don't know what I'd do to comfort him, to prove to him that, despite everything, I always did, really did, love him. Oh, God, Beth, I really did love him, I do love him, present tense, and yes, that's what I want: I want to go." She cups her mouth with her hand, and I nearly hear her sob.

"Okay," I say, breathing hard, catching myself so that I don't cry, too. "Then there's no excuse. You're going, okay? You're going to board that plane and go. Take him the pictures, Andrée. Show him. He'll know." *Trust me. Believe me. Let me help you through this. Please.*

"Greek," she says. "Right? Didn't I say Greek?" She forces a finger under her glasses and brushes the wetness away. She looks at me. She needs to know that I am telling her the truth.

"Greek is fine," I say, looking back at her, all honesty. "We'll take my car," I say, and I don't look for my scarf. It doesn't matter anymore.

"I'm going to eat bread," the little girl says, clutching her Beanie Baby for dear life. "Since I can't have cereal, I'm having bread."

"Bread is good," I say. "They'll have plenty of bread, and you can have as much as you want. A loaf full, a table full, a room full of bread. Anything, anything you want."

II

Being There

I GO HOME, and nothing is as it was. The sound of my shoes in the hallway a reckoning. The photographs in their dusty glass traps straining to speak, empty of promises. It is impossible not to feel Andrée's pain, not to bring it here, not to cloak myself in it, so that it, along with my footsteps, puts its weight, its sound, inside the house. Puts out a light.

Nothing is as it was. Is it that I am nearly forty and life just now, this winter thawing to spring, has snapped my friends into its grip? It isn't, face it, just Andrée. It is one friend's divorce, another friend's addiction, another's disappointment, and yet another's pileup of losses—her father first, then her mother. It is —go back, be brave, stare it in the face—Andrée. Nobody should have to hurt this badly, fear this deeply, lose this unilaterally, and yet she has, she will, and here's the lesson: empathy is a terrible deception. Empathy is imagining myself to be Andrée while I walk the rooms of my own resolute house and absentmindedly conquer the clutter. I marinate the steak for my son and my husband, who is, for now, healthy, who will come home and kiss the salty ledge of my cheek and spoon his knees into mine at night because he knows that words don't do the healing. Empathy is empty, a float above reality. I am here in a peaceful place, and Andrée is in her own house, with her own children, with her own husband dying on a South Korean hill. Empathy is Andrée's pain in the lines of my face, Andrée's pain, not mine, settling in.

Five years ago I moved one hour west from Andrée, after she had spent six years answering the words that yearned in me. I have profitably gone from the old neighborhood, and now others, in my absence, are no doubt showing up on Andrée's sloping, shoe-worn stoop to take their stations and do the corporal, credible labor of friendship. Lynn: wise, Germanic, pragmatic. The Koreans with their bundles of herbs. Donna, who will no doubt occupy the younger kids with play. The minister who, on behalf of the congregation, will bring money enough for the time being. The neighbor who lives in my once and never house will take care of the seedy strip of garden that Andrée once took care of for my sake, just for me. Andrée's mother will come in the toil and bang of her concern and will nonetheless stay on until her daughter can make it on her own.

If you think friendship is an organ of convenience, think again: it takes its toll. As we grow older, there will be more of life to take head on or divert or despise or explain. Hands will reach out, hours will be consumed, voices won't go dim in the night. In the crowd that gathers around every life, in the friendships that close in on every heartbreak, there will be martyrs and saints, sprinters and marathoners, those too poor to offer up gifts, those too busy to give one more fraction of time. There will be a little *watch-me-do-this*. A little *I-am-the-hero*. A little *come-on-now-what-about-me?* Open hearts will become burdened hearts will become overtaxed and grumbling hearts, and some will start to wonder out loud how long they can go on with the fatiguing job of caring. How long *should* they? What are the rules? What proves a friendship? How much of oneself is for giving away? Define selfishness, define self-preservation. Find the wholly selfless one among us. Someone needs to write down what we owe one another; what we, *without a second's pause*, should give; what we'll later regret not giving. Someone needs to quantify the human capacity for concern, for going beyond oneself, into the graceland of giving, which is another way of saying friendship. Pure.

Or if, here again, language fails us, we need to take the living lessons from the standard-bearers among us, those who imagine their way into friendship, take a stance against loss, and make a difference. This is the winter that is relieved not by the news but by the surpassing kindness of friends. The season in which I have finally learned that tragedy is random. How we respond to it is not.

Jamie calls. A friend of hers, younger than me, is dying. He has children. She is going to see him, she says, and she wants to bring gifts. We talk for a while about the options. She decides on her own that she will buy books for his sons. She will choose them and wrap them and give them to her friend, so that he in turn can present them to his children. Jamie will imagine what her friend would do if he could get out to the stores, out of his cancer.

Amy sends a note: her aunt is dying. There is a letter-writing campaign afoot, she says; everyone who ever knew her aunt is to harvest and write down their memories. Memories of a favorite Passover meal. Memories of a favorite private joke. Memories of victories and gallantries, small points of beauty. Memories for Amy and her cousins to read to the woman who is fading so quickly. Memories for them to keep afterward, when what they loved has passed away from this earth.

Tom, who rarely calls, has called. His life's been changed, he says. He can't get his footing. A friend has died, leaving behind a widow and a son, and Tom wants to do what he can. Wants to perform some kind of miracle so that the widow will survive, so that the child won't forget his father, so that the house in which that family lived will not be a fortress of grief. Tom has taken on the papers and the tax forms, the banks, the law, but it is not enough, he says, it's inconsequential. The widow still goes to sleep alone, the infant will not know his father's voice, Tom's good friend is still gone. I can't make this better, Tom says, so he tries harder, does more than anybody can.

Joanne, I say in an e-mail, *they're falling hard around these parts, and I don't know what to do.* She writes back: *I get confused about this too, you know; most everybody does. Though there's always my husband, who just opens his wallet, asks how much is needed, doles out cash, and then goes right on to the next thing, unencumbered by bad news. I don't think,* Joanne writes, *that he is ever really worried. He knows that he's done what he can.*

Reflecting on all this, wondering what others can do for friends in times of trouble, and how much difference it makes, I see myself at twenty-six. I am newly married and long gone from the office of unfriendlies. I've become an entrepreneur, with a list of sixteen firms in my consulting portfolio, and at last my iconoclasm and speed are not just welcomed and congratulated but paid for. In the day I hurry across the city from office to office, setting up architectural marketing systems, writing brochures, teaching secretaries the mechanics of cold calls. At night Bill and I, squeezed into Camac Street's third-floor suite, oblige each other's artistic temperaments by rotating ownership of the inadequate front room. He paints in the "studio" from midnight to four, and when the cats start clinking trash cans, I come down the hallway and kiss him goodnight. He kisses me and travels in reverse and crashes into bed. Sitting on the floor of the front room, I find my muse and start to write. At dawn I eat a cookie. At eight I wake Bill, and day begins.

And then one dawn, breaking my store-bought cookies into palatable chunks, I realize I am chewing with my tongue. I put my pen down and try to use my teeth, but the apparatus is on strike. My bottom teeth are boycotting engagement with the top. Alarmed, I go to the bathroom, blink at the mirror. My face doesn't look the way it should.

Probably the hinge of my jaw has been unscrewing for months; it simply took my lusting after a cookie for me to notice. For a couple of weeks I pretend that the machinery of my mouth will up and fix itself. When it looks hopeless, I see a doctor and get news I find appalling. It's a genetic deformity; surgery is required. But first, can I say *ahh* for a pair of braces? Just the thing for a new bride, and now I come home and I'm unlovely.

Bill keeps on painting, I keep consulting. We move to a trinity near South Street. November comes, the surgery is scheduled, and I'm in a miserable mood. I won't be able to speak for ten weeks. I won't be able to eat. And they're planning to sever a facial nerve that can't grow back, so I won't ever again feel the full embrace of Bill's sweet kiss. That, to me, is the greatest misfortune. Remembering this now, I put my finger to my lip. Yes, it never did regain its feeling.

Though it is cold enough for snow, rain has been falling for days, a gray slush in a steel city that Bill and I tramp through, hand in hand, on the day I'm to check in for surgery. At the front desk, Bill takes care of all the nagging little details, while I practice what it will be like not to talk. I check in to my room and meet my roommate, who is half-dressed and filthy, her face newly cudgeled with the butt of a gun. Barbara has a thirteen-year-old daughter, and her one-year-old grandson is running a truck across her bed. Bill stays with me, then it's night and he goes home. And then it is dawn, and there are needles.

They roll me away. I feel the cold fit of the catheter. I see the tubes they'll slide down my nose, and the buckets to catch the blood. I hear somebody say, *We're finally going to get that mouth right, Beth. We're going to fix that jaw. You'll be able to chew again, eat real food, now what do you think about that?* I hear somebody counting backward above my head, and when I wake again, I feel a drowning terror: my whole mouth is clamped shut, my face pulpy as fruit, the tubes in my nose obstructing the air that I need; I must get a swallow of air. There's no way to speak, and they've tied my hands to the bed, and now the white sheets go red, the color of rubies. And now I am slipping beneath the sea of red, and hands are all around me, enclosing me, mopping me, correcting the tubes, saying, *You're fine. You're just fine now. We're pumping the blood from your stomach. This is the machine. This is how it works. We've changed your sheets.* Someone asks a question, and the voice comes back: *It was harder than we planned for. We lost a lot of blood.* I don't understand, and I have no way of saying so, but my family is near — my mother, my father, my sister, Bill — monitoring the pumps and tubes, smoothing down the fresh sheets, talking to me softly, taking care.

They allow Bill to stay until midnight. Because of the holidays, the hospital is short-staffed, and the nurses are glad for the extra pair of hands, for someone to supervise the machine that keeps clogging, keeps sending the blood in wrong directions, a red gash across my chin, red gash upon the pillow. How many fresh pillowcases will Bill have to scrounge for me tonight? From across the curtains, I hear Barbara say that she can help, that she had the same "funked" machine stuffed down her gut and she knows its "goddamned kinky" process. Then the nurse says it's time for Bill to go, the worst is over, the machine is running well. He says he'll be back, and then it's just Barbara and me, and the rain outside that has turned to snow. *Hot damn, girl, look over here and watch the snow.*

All that night I think I am drowning, and all that night Barbara is there, saving my life. Talking and talking, asking unanswerable questions, chronicling her life, telling me stories of the bar at Forty-sixth and Arch, where she, a few nights before, was mercilessly clobbered. With her jaw broken in three places and most of her teeth rocked from their sockets, her tongue is loose in her mouth, and I can't sleep. But I also won't drown, because Barbara knows what to do, she's got a talent for keeping the pump machine working. *Hot damn, girl, I got you. Hot damn, girl, you're fine.* By the end of the night, Barbara has settled down on my bed. She's fixing the machine, reporting snow. Within a few hours Bill comes and takes up his post. I sleep after that for an hour or two, and when I wake, my half of the room is roaring: a jungle of flowers.

It is, without question, a most glorious sight: here, in living silks of color, the friends I have, a sweet aroma.

A few days later, I leave the hospital, making sure to collect Barbara's address, making sure that she has her share of flowers. After a few days at my mother's, where I luxuriate in her care and also learn that you can vomit through your nose, Bill and I head home.

It is true, as the doctors had warned: I cannot eat, I cannot speak. The best I can do is run a straw up to one tooth and suck and suck until some milk weeps its way through. I look like an inverted pumpkin, my head twice its natural size, my five-foot-four body down to eighty-four pounds and dropping precariously. But here's the strange thing: these are very good days. I would not trade them for the world. My friends send more flowers. They bring me presents. They call and talk at me on the phone. My husband proves that he can love me no matter how grotesque I look, and I make my mother laugh, and I tell my sister, finally, with an invention of sign language, that I love her. Then Nazie, my gorgeous Persian friend, comes to visit in a blowing winter storm. She sits on the couch and reports her travel adventures, while I write letters on a pad she's brought me from a paper maker near Florence.

Nazie, your beauty is what I remember. Your laughter. Your waiting for my words.

A few months after we moved away from Andrée, Bambi found her way into our lives. There is a little red-doored, white-planked church with a tall plain steeple not far from here, the sort of church that comes directly from the nursery rhyme. Hand in hand one Sunday morning, Jeremy and I set off to explore it. We went upstairs and downstairs, pressing our noses against Sunday school windows. We sat through the sermon, sang with the songs, read along in the Bible, shook the minister's warm hand, then toured the classrooms again, leaving breath marks on the interior glass. I suppose Bambi noticed our touring expedition, and I remember watching her excuse herself from the fellowship-hour crowd to make her way over to Jeremy and me. "This is a good place," she said, her tone blessedly matter-of-fact and not evangelical. "My three kids have grown up here, and we're happy with the memories we've got."

"Well, that's great," I said. "Good to know."

A petite, no-fuss lady, Bambi now made herself even smaller to gain Jeremy's trust. "So tell me about you," she asked, her eyes at his level. "What are you looking to find here?"

"Cars," Jeremy said stutteringly, shy. "I like cars." He was five at the time, and he'd told the truth.

"This is the place for you, then," Bambi told him, affirmingly, as if miniature cars were on everyone's church prerequisite list. "You're in luck. Check this out." She raised her fragile arm with its tower of bracelets and pointed to a mix-up of plastic Corvettes and mini gas trucks in one corner of the nearest room. Jeremy raised an eyebrow in approval, then hid, again shy, in my skirts. "Wait till you meet my kids," Bambi told the part of him she could still see. "And wait till you meet my dog. He wants to come to church with us, but we're old fogies: we don't let him."

You expect that a whole church is going to welcome you in, but church is just like everything else, it's person by person, and slowly. Bambi, after that first encounter, never forgot to be our friend. I liked the occasional *damn* in her sentences, her appealing irreverence, her loud making-of-room for Jeremy and me in her already family-filled pew. Once, when asked to introduce us on New Member Sunday, she forged ahead and hand-fashioned the details—stood there with a straight face and told that Presbyterian congregation things she couldn't possibly know about my Catholic husband, my miniature house, the work I do, Jeremy's favorite foods. Jeremy started smirking in midcourse. I held my own in my high-collared dress. Ringing her tower of bracelets, she finished her fictions and turned to deliver a wink. A relative stranger. An intimate joke. The consolidation of a friendship between us.

What I know about Bambi has been whispered between the Doxology and the Apostle's Creed, passed down during Christmas pageants, handed off in the shallow cradle of chatter. More to the point, it's been observed. I know her fierce devotion to family by watching her family's devotion to her. I know the depth of her humanity by watching how blue her eyes burn during the best of the sermons. I know that her life bears its own tumescent pain, but I also know, because I've noticed, that she will not dwell on the damage she's sustained. Bambi's not one to let on when her heart is throbbing, not one to ask, not one to need. One day in the early season of Andrée's suffering, Bambi told me something about her good friend Jeffrey. He was dying, she said. He would never be more than sixteen. She had held him and known him since he had come into the world; she had been, from the start, his godmother. Now a tumor was blooming like a flower in his brain. Tubes were doing all his living for him. Bit by bit, in a city hospital, his sixty trillion cells were dying while the tumor dug in its roots, and in the shadows and in the light, Bambi was there.

I could picture her in the hospital room, holding her godson's hand, rattling her bracelets, saying *damn* a thousand times so that he would hear and would know who had come to pass the time. She was probably talking about her dog or about J.R.R. Tolkien, or about how her one son had hit a homer and her other a hole in one, how her daughter was filling the house up with flute sounds. She was probably saying, *Jeff, you are braver than anyone I've ever known,* then going right back out to the newsreel of life in defiance of all those tubes. To the latest movies, another book, to headlines, more dog stories, promises: *Your parents love you, Jeff. You will never be forgotten.* What do you talk about at the very end, in the relentless paralysis of grief? How do you sit in the company of torment and make the present moment count? I said empathy is empty, but it doesn't have to be. Empathy is Jamie, Amy, Tom. It's Bambi, knowing what to do.

Dying has no regard for the life it claims, nor does it consider those on its fringe. It isn't orderly, it sneers at schedules. It's left to the living to figure it out, to pattern the compassion, the concern, the extensions. The mother and father take turns sleeping in the hospital beside their son at night. The siblings appear in the afternoons. Grandparents are cautioned to come when they can. In the crush and crawl of living through the dying, there are those who will apply their intelligence against the assault of chaos. Those who, like Bambi, will silently slip in as backup, cooking meals for the family, leaving fresh groceries on the stoop, driving the expressway many days of every week and finding, among all those tubes, her given godson's hand. I'm not sure how much of what she did was noticed, or how much she would have confessed to me, an outsider, had not something in our conversation cracked and opened. I had been looking for signs of selflessness in friendship, looking for standards, and in Bambi, the anti-saint, I found them.

On Good Friday, Bambi gave her godson his final memory of scripture. I wasn't there, I didn't see it. I can only imagine it through the story I asked Bambi to tell because I wanted, somehow, to join her in worship. *It took four of us close to four hours*, she told me, *to bathe Jeff, to dress Jeff, to sit him safely in his wheelchair.* She was speaking of nurses, I guess, of herself, maybe of Jeff's father. She was leading up to the fact that Jeff was religious, that this teenager fighting three years of cancer had managed to cling to his faith, and that Bambi, knowing that, wanted to honor him and honor it. She wanted to give him what she believed he would ask for, if he could only stop dying and speak. Bambi had told the minister of our church and he, a good man, had promptly stopped all other business and sat down and written Jeff a service. Bambi had taken it to the hospital that last Good Friday with the idea of dressing Jeff, releasing him, taking him down the hall and into the elevator and then down another hall and out into the hospital's urban garden. It was cloudy, but there were flowers, and among the yellow and red of the petals, Bambi found Jeff a sacred spot. Kneeling down, finding his hand, she read about a man and a cross and resurrection. My mind's eye leaves her story right there: two friends in a garden, in a shroud of weather. Two friends in a garden, holding hands. In just a few days, Jeff's body would disappear completely, but what remains, and always will, is this kneeling down in prayer.

I write to Andrée late at night. I worry, I say, at how my imagination has failed me. I tell her that I know Lynn has come, and Donna, that Korean herbs and antidotes are stacking up in her front hall, that neighbors are pitching in, doing their part. I know about the ministrations of the church, the acquisition of a visa, the procurement of a single airline pass. I know that Andrée's mother is finally on her way, so that Andrée can be on her way to South Korea.

If there is a seam that hasn't been sewn, tell me the color of its thread.

The electronic words twitch surreally on my screen. I read them through a second time and click the arrow on Send. Andrée is not a friend I should be reaching through wires, and I feel deeply nostalgic for the sound of her footsteps on my porch, the rush of night air, the airmail-size envelopes, the loopy ink on transparent onionskin, the parenthetical force of the paper's folds. I am nostalgic for all of that, but there it is: we are older now, our lives have changed. There it is: I'm this far away, and it's late, and there's no running my worry to her doorstep, a pot of marigolds in my hands.

In bed I am restless, alone. Bill is in the basement making art, and Jeremy, down the hall, is dreaming his dreams. I crack the pleats of the blinds with one finger and go eyeball to eyeball with the moon. Three-quarters full, it does not blink. It holds its weight above the trees. Bambi's godson is out there, I think, and Amy's aunt, Jamie's friend, the widow's husband, mingling with so many escapees, roving the hundred billion galaxies, skimming the edge of a vortex. A star forms. A star burns. A star swallows itself whole, its whisper terminating in nervous impulses and dust.

Drawn to my own breathing, the loudest sound in the room, I am struck, as I so often am, by the wonder of my life here on earth. By the web of providence and implausibility that formed my cells and instructed my genes and endowed me with friendships, family. This is my life, and this is my window, and this is my version of the moon, hanging there, swelling in all its glory,

either an accident or an invention—make your choice. I have
made mine.

No birth is easy, and the birth of the moon required the cleav-
ing of our planet, the giving up of one thing for the yielding of
another. Think of an outrageous planetesimal zinging trillions
of miles across the universe and striking the earth, just like that.
Think of five billion cubic miles of basalt and granite spewing
upward, fast, into outer space, and think of the millennia upon
millennia it took for all that earthly debris to gather itself into
the rock we call the moon. The moon hovered close after it was
born. So close, some scientists say, that every tide was a tsunami,
every day/night cycle a mere six hours long.   Imagine that.
Imagine the steaming, hissing, settling earth overtaken by a sky
full of moon. Only by infinitesimal increments did the moon
start gaining some distance, so that even today, four billion years
after its birth, it remains inextricably bound to the earth.

Because of the moon, the earth slowed on its axis and made
room for the likes of us. Because of the moon, there is a brilliant
mathematics to the tides. Because of the moon, our skies remind
us every evening that we are made more powerful by the things
we give away.

Back here on earth it's the dawn of a new millennium. We are
all in our own private houses, in our rooms, in relative nearness
and farness from the people we love, the friends who have
soaked into our families, into our hearts, and we are wondering,
and worrying, and, if we pray, we are praying, and if we are
Jamie, Amy, Tom, or Bambi, if we are Barbara or Nazie, or my
husband or my sister, my mother, we are knowing what to do. I
suspect that Andrée's children are in bed by now, and that she
has left her porch light on, and that there's a hot bulb in the

kitchen, a bag of unopened clementines on the table. If she is the woman I believe she is, Andrée is sitting at her kitchen table, a Bible on her lap, her ear tuned to the phone she hopes will ring and, like a miracle, reverse her husband's news.

Send me a sign, I urge her from where I lie in bed. *Tell me how you are tonight*. From down the hall, Jeremy sighs. The moon doesn't blink. The trees stretch their naked branches out into the night like dendrites.

12

Snapping

Discontent festers deep within the earth. Down where we can't see it, beyond the loam, the limestone, the granite, the shale, down where the earth is still a beast, roaring and roiling, where mountains hang like stalactites from the bottom of the mantle, and the hot, slathering melt of iron flows across the upside-down and airless peaks. The earth is as hot as hell, tormented, still forming. Up here we're all on rafts, our continents drifting together, inch by yearly inch, our civilizations dodging the white-hot plumes that spew from the center of the earth.

We live on fragments on an entirely fragile crust; we are exposed to the serendipity of the sky. Houses, music, passions, and also friendships provide a patterning calm despite all the evidence to the contrary, all the rocks moving at our feet, all the gasping metals. But friendship too can become its own puissant chaos, the shattering antithesis of calm. A knot instead of a lifeline. An overturned bottle of beads. *These are very Old Testament days*, a friend of mine says, and she isn't speaking just of the weather or indiscriminate politics or guns in our schools or the slaughter of innocents. I no longer run to get the mail. I'm no longer eager when the phone rings. I no longer trust what I will hear when a friend gets on the line.

"Are you okay?" Lately I've learned to ask the question first. And suddenly, this winter, in shocking succession, the answer is too often, *No.* These days, often, I find that another friend is under siege. Here is my new neighbor, inexpressibly sad. Here are two others headed for divorce. Here is a friend who is out of a job, a friend who's been betrayed, one who misses her father, another who misses her marriage, another whose child is at risk, another who can't find the wisdom to parent. Here is a friend who has to move and a friend who can't, and here are the tumors, the cancers, the rare blood disorders that are blasting the light out of people. Here are the unfulfilled and the dissatisfied, the unacknowledged and the guilty, the disrespected and the underserved, and all of that, *all of it*, deserves an answer, a dwelling place. An end bracket. A plug. All of it deserves more than most of us can give.

These days, in self-defense, I've started to put my friends' woes on a clock, to niche and nook them, assign them certain days of the week. *I am available*, I tell them, and I allot each one an hour, and I apply my whole self, conscientiously, for that hour, and then I'm on to the next friend and the next, taking their adversities in sequence, putting books in the mail, flowers at the door. I'm in the store buying cards and mailing them on schedule, as if compassion could be calendared and purchased. Or I build a hierarchy of sensitivity, intervention, follow-through, that shares an equivalency with the debts I owe or the relative severity of their personal hardships. Or I let every ounce of turmoil and pain whack itself together, to mass big and dark and knock me down, so that I'm immobile and speechless. I'm here without my skin, and my pages are blank, and my son drifts out of view, and my husband, when he reaches to find me at night, finds nothing but my soreness and my need. *Tell me about yourself,* I whisper to Bill, and he says, *No, you are too full of all those other people's problems.* We lie then in the quiet, and he holds my hand, and I am relieved and sorry that he must retreat to give me room. I am relieved and sorry that my best friend, my husband, is wreathing his arms around me so that tomorrow I'll have what it takes to reach back out to others.

All of us need a place to which we can turn our hearts. When the circle of compassion breaks, the results are catastrophic. Jeremy, listen to this. Jeremy, I want you to know.

A long time ago I was acquainted with a family whose members for the most part weren't related by blood. To be sure, Julie had a nuclear, genetic family, three beautiful born-and-bred children. But for the most part her family was an extension of developmentally disabled adults—a whirligig of misfits for whom making friends was life's great challenge. Julie, in essence, had brought these grownups home. During the day her business, as a minimally paid job coach, was to help adults with every imaginable disadvantage find jobs and learn how to keep them. During the evenings, and on weekends and holidays, Julie and her kids stepped into their lives as virtually the only friends that they had.

It was the idea of their Christmases that had me most seduced. When Julie described them, I felt that I had been there myself in her modest flat above an old town's Main Street, watching her stir the pasta on the stove. I imagined it all into present tense. I imagined Jason, with his camcorder and side-long glance, his burnished, perseverative tales of babies, diapers, sex. Robert, sullenly relieved to be included, furious with a pair of hands that had never done him much good. Mark, bound up in a self-referential circle of talk, and Lynn, the effervescent one —her moon face catching the glint of the room's twinkle lights and burning candles, the orange street lamps and illuminated decorations that bobbed outside in the winter dark like buoys. Dancing, Lynn would be. Dancing, smacking her body up against the potbelly stove and the bright blue, apple-laden table and the street signs and advertisements and jade plants and the little porcelain Buddha that glittered in Julie's perpetually crowded flat. It was Christmas at Julie's house, and the Partridge Family would be crowing from the boom box, while Lynn shim-mied and grooved, ramming her sweaty glasses up the short bridge of her nose, flicking away the thin strands of her dark hair. *Chulie, Chulie, Chulie,* Lynn would call, and Julie would hear her and smile from across the room, where she was check-ing the pasta, or discouraging a brawl among her cats, or help-ing her son through a taxing word in the book he was reading while his sisters washed dishes and Robert sulked and Jason videotaped and Lynn remained in her delighted outrage of dance.

Julie's guests were refugees. They were family. Jason, with anorexia and a most severe obsessive-compulsive disorder. Robert, who did not learn to read until he was sixty-five, when Julie sat him down and taught him how. Mark, his brain myste-riously dented, his weakness being trust in mankind, a naiveté that prevented him from knowing when and how to cross a street, when and how to yield his money, when and how to make babies out of love. Lynn, with Down syndrome and odd, double-jointed limbs, and a little girl's dream of marrying a painter and conceiving and raising ten smart kids. I was around Jason, Robert, Mark, Lynn for a long time. I paid attention, but I did not see what was coming.

I was seduced. I loved the illusion of parity embedded in these friendships. I loved the way Julie would visit with Lynn at her parents' house, shushing away the concerns of Lynn's mother, who never seemed to forget that this was not the child she'd planned for. Lynn told Julie her secrets in a high giggle, talked to her about boys, showed off her new culottes and Keds. Once, near Halloween, I met Julie at Lynn's parents' low-slung ranch house; when I got there, late, Julie and Lynn were comfortably arranged on the front-room couch in a room that smelled like lit-up pumpkins. They were hanging there, I remember, in the absolute balance of friendship—Lynn tangling her fingers in the pleats of Julie's unruly hair and clapping explosively to release small jolts of joy. Small-boned and fragile, but for the rupture of cobalt eyes, Julie was recounting stories, jogging Lynn's memory, boasting quietly about the job Lynn had then held for more than a year—a job in corporate America, an answer to a prayer. Now and then Julie would stretch her arm across the expanse of Lynn's shoulders, an incontrovertible demonstration of her heart. Lynn would shiver and kink and bend in toward Julie, amazed and embarrassed, renewed, suddenly self-confident. It looked like weaving. It looked like comfort. A dish of October candy was passed from lap to lap.

Later, Lynn's parents still hovering in the back of the house, the three of us clopped down to the basement, where Lynn

cranked up an old Partridge Family song and snapped and exer-
cised to the chirpy beat while Julie, her hair in a tumble around
her shoulders, softly sang along to the tune. In time Lynn spread
a hooped and brightly threaded tablecloth on the basement
floor and explained to Julie, behind the wall of music, that the
embroidered linen was a gift-in-the-making for a friendly lady
next door. Straightening up, she tossed darts across the room,
calling out, in a harmless vendetta, the names of those each sil-
ver-pointed prick was for. Then she sat down proudly before her
computer and navigated the Net—a certain ingenious pluck as
both her compass and her guide.

But what endured when the evening was over, when the full
moon outside had levered down past the horizon, was the
wholesome quality of this friendship, the dish of candy that became a running joke. What remained was my own errant question: "Lynn, who are you, really?"

"I'm Down syndrome," she answered, the consonants clotted,
the vowel sounds flat, the mounded shoulders rising up and
falling in a long and disappointed shrug. "I'm frenely. I'm goot
to people. I'm accractive. But I'm Down syndrome."

It was an awkward breach of language, and the room was utterly still, and then Julie, visibly unsettled and sad, found the
words with which to redress the balance. "Down syndrome is
just a fragment of who you are, Lynn," she said emphatically.
"The tiniest sliver."

"Oh, Chulie," Lynn answered, huge sighs, ten fingers flying.
"Oh, Chulie," both arms wide and high above her head, then
thrown heavily across the shoulders of her friend.

This friendship had a history and a future. It had begun in a
daycare, essentially, for adults with disabilities, where Julie had

gone to help keep the peace after years of doing every other imaginable odd job. They'd tended tomatoes together, Julie and Lynn, cranking up the Frank Sinatra, swaying in the sunshine, dreaming out loud about some distant time when Lynn could have a real job in a real place where the real employees wore real shoes. Over the years Julie changed jobs and pulled Lynn up along with her—finding her a spot as a mail room clerk in a fancy banking outfit and training her to do it, training her to get there, rooting for her as Lynn, with her own unique brand of fierce intelligence, did not just succeed but soared.

"To be honest-est-est?" Lynn told me that night near Halloween. "When I gut the job news from Chulie I said to mysouf, Lynn, now you know there is a Gott."

"Were we ever happy," Julie said, squeezing Lynn's hand. "Did we ever smile. And you should have seen this lady on her very first day. Pantyhose, deodorant, cologne, she had it all. She looked great in the front seat of my car."

"Because Chulie, she drove me the first day." Lynn was speaking over her friend. "Because I was nervous-ous-ous, really nervous-ous-ous. I taut to mysouf I'll get lost in that beg building. I woan find my way around-round-round. No one will talk to me, I taut. And I'll tell you something. I want to be honest, tell you the truth. I could not haff done it without my friend Chulie. I could not haff. I could not haff. I would not haff. Not ever. And now I'm vewy vewy proud of me. I haff a chob. I'm independann. I can do it by mysouf. And I can do it because of Chulie."

Julie got Lynn her job, and she went on to transform the stuck lives of Jason, of Mark, of Robert, of a dozen more—all of whom became her friends, part of her family. They came for dinner. They called on the phone. They were adopted by Julie's three teenage children. It was exhilarating and, of course, it was exhausting. Julie had to work a second job to pay for the food and the flat and the accoutrements of family. *She's always working,* her kids would tell me when I called to check in. *She's running herself into the ground. And when she's home, she's always on the phone with them. One of them, always, needs something.*

Which was true—anyone could see it. As much as Julie loved her friends, as reciprocal and equitable as all those good feelings were, the *burden* of those relationships, the base responsibilities, amassed on two small shoulders. The more Julie was there for Jason, the more he needed her praise, her approval, her forgiveness. The more Julie intervened on behalf of Robert, the more interventions he grew to expect. The more Mark loved the job that Julie had found him, the more he needed her to find him another when the first was gone, and when the next one also vanished. The more Julie elevated Lynn's sense of self and potential, the more Lynn needed to hear an answer, be given a promise: *Tell me I can liff with you, Chulie, when my parents die. Tell me you're going to be here for me, so that I am not alone.*

A few weeks after Halloween, I spent an evening with Julie in her quirky above-Main-Street flat. She had taken the night off from her second job at a library, and she was home with her children and her cats, ensconced at the kitchen table, sewing something retro for her sixteen-year-old daughter. A grandfather clock provided news of the night while Julie's son sat at the table doing homework, glancing up at quarter-hour intervals. The two older girls ran up and down the steps, finally settling in with us over cups of tea. The phone rang twice; it was Jason, and Julie calmed him down. Then Lynn checked in and Robert called. In

between phone calls, Julie and I talked about family. We talked about how all of this had started. We talked about getting in so deep that her life had stopped being her own.

"They call because they call," Julie told me that night. "They want to tell me about their day. Who else, honestly, are they going to talk to? Who else will understand their little victories or defeats? They have a job. They have their stories. It's not like they're going home to a spouse."

"They call too much," one daughter said, her sigh exasperated. "I mean, they're nice and all, but Mom..."

"Well, Robert's angry," Julie had defended, "and you would be, too. Someone else has to tie his apron, and his brother won't invite him for Thanksgiving, and his housemate eats more than he should. So he calls to talk, and I feel sorry, and I listen. And Mark, you know, he's one of my favorites. I don't mind listening to his dreams."

"Mark says the same thing every time he calls," the second daughter chimed in. "Same thing, like a record." She looked at me to plead her case. "He calls my mom to tell her, and it's the same thing, every time."

"He's just dreaming out loud about his big wedding day, and I don't see that there's much harm in listening," Julie countered.

"There isn't," the boy put in his two cents, "if you have nothing else to do."

"Mom had to get a night job so she wouldn't be on the phone all the time," the older daughter teased, her voice sardonic. By this time the tea had gone cold.

"I had to get a night job to pay for your tuition," Julie told her. "And don't you forget it, Miss Missy."

. . .

Through weeks, through many months, I got to know Julie rather well. We ate lunch together; she called me; she told me more about her life. My original impressions of her goodness held fast but also broadened as I struggled to reconcile her alternative psycho-philosophies with her marketing acumen, her roguish behavior within her own company's bureaucracy with her flat-out commitment to her assortment of clients. She talked about books and seemed to read good ones. She talked about her children with a vast, liberal love. She talked about the ironies of corporate America with cynical turns of phrase, sparing no one who got in her way. "I go to these corporations with a decent job-creation proposal and they flat-out turn me down," she told me at one point. "I am sitting there offering the world's most loyal employees, promising personally to do all the training, all the troubleshooting, all the settling in. But even that doesn't turn most of these companies' heads. After a while, it runs you down. That and my boss," she said, conspiratorially, "but I'm not going to go into that."

Talking to Julie yielded powerful glimpses into essential, gentle equations. She remembered her first days with Lynn — tending zucchinis, singing "My Way," trading fantasies. She revealed more about Jason — telling how, in those first crucial days of his job, she spent hours in his employer's parking lot calming him down. She talked about Robert and all the good years he'd lost because no one had believed he could read. She told stories about Mark's interminable bus ride, stuck on "the whole God damned hot bus route" because he hadn't the skills to cross a street on his own. "Mark lives just a few blocks from his job," she confided. "And the stupid thing is that he sits on that bus for an hour until it turns around and drops him off at the restaurant's curb."

"So you rode the bus with him?" I wondered.

"Of course. That's how he learned."

"Every day, the same route?"

"Me and Mark and the girl he wants to marry in the church that he can't stop talking about."

"You're kidding."

"No I'm not. That's what I do. These are my friends. These are their lives. No one else is looking out for them, and I can't let them down."

"So who's doing something for you, Julie?" I asked her.

She waved her hand in the air to scat the question off.

But that, as it turns out, was the question that most mattered. That is the question that, had it been answered to any smidgen of satisfaction, might have saved Julie and her assortment of kin from what happened next, the high, devastating drama I somehow didn't see coming. As time went on, Julie's unwieldy family grew increasingly taxing. As time went on, there weren't enough phones in the house, enough money in the bank, enough hours in the day for all their cares and possibilities. Everything good was flowing out from Julie's hands. Nothing substantive was flowing back in. Julie's family was wacky and happy and safe until Julie, airlessly trapped in the heart of it all, learned for sure that she had no place to go. That her own small ambition had not been answered. That she had overextended, burned up, reached too wide with her net of friendships. That what she'd wanted for herself had been squelched by a bureaucracy. That was the day my own phone rang, the day when it all, in one unsalvageable instant, snapped and fell apart.

I was aware of the winter rain knocking on my windows and

of Julie's voice, strangely outside itself—a pitch, a vein, that was alien.

"Jesus," she started. "Shit. I can't do it. I can't. It's all over." There was disgust in her voice, a foreign sound, a visceral splattering of her heart.

"What happened?" I asked, putting my book down, taken about. "What are you talking about? What's wrong?"

"My daughter's tuition is on a credit card," she blurted out, an apparent tangent to which I had no reply. "I'm behind on the bills; I'm exhausted."

"I know you are," I offered. "You need a break." I wanted to calm her down. "No one can keep on keeping on."

"I didn't get it," she said. "I work my ass off. They passed me by."

"You didn't get what?" I tried to understand. I pedaled backward in my mind. *Who passed her by?*

"The promotion. My boss. Says I'm not a team player, then passes me by. It's all I wanted, Beth," she said. "All I wanted. I could have stopped working both jobs. I could have breathed. I could have slept. It was all I wanted. It was the something for *me*."

"I'm sorry," I said. "I really am. You should be queen, the way you work. You should be..."

"*Not a team player*, the boss says, and smack in the middle of him explaining this to me, Robert calls—mad as hell, out on a limb. Everything I drop for him—*everything I drop*, and then I'm out in this weather, driving, looking for Robert, finding him, pacing, in the parking lot. In the pouring rain, he's pacing. Out there with his apron on, pissed off about this thing and that, and all I could think of is, Jesus Christ, I've got pain, too, and the rain is hard as ice."

"I'm sorry, Julie."

"It's over."

"What do you mean?" I asked, not understanding, not hearing, not broaching the depth of her anger. I see that all in retrospect—that I did not understand how far out on the rocky cliff she was. I hadn't stopped to worry, in any meaningful way, about who reached out to her, who kept her intact. "What are you saying?"

"I'm saying I can't fix Jason's obsessions and I can't find Lynn a painter and I don't know if Mark's going to have his day at church. I'm saying that I'm not standing in the rain anymore trying to mend these broken hearts, and what kind of bullshit is that, that I'm not a team player, and how the hell am I supposed to come clean with my credit cards? I'm lousy worn out and I'm at the end of my rope, and I'm not going back there. I'm saying what I'm saying. It's all over. I'm not the person I thought I was."

"Tomorrow you'll wake up and this will look different."

"Tomorrow I'll wake up and the only way it will be different is if I do what I'm saying. It's over."

"You can't just quit." I was almost yelling now. "You can't, Julie. You quit, a whole world comes crashing down." I was thinking about all the shatterable links in the tenuous chain. I was thinking about Lynn's thumb-sized fingers in Julie's spritzy hair, about Jason's twice-a-day phone calls. "You said it yourself. You are responsible. They slip up, they're out. Who's going to keep them on their feet? And besides, Julie. Besides. They are your friends, and you are theirs. You are the only friend they've got. You are their Christmas."

"It's over, Beth," she told me. "It's over. They'll have to find somebody else."

· · ·

I have a friend who is a charter member of the Original Cookie Exchange, a socialist society of well-off suburban moms, a private club of roll-your-sleeves-up women who for the past ten years have specialized in serving one another. A grueling point system guides their ministrations. If you want something—a reprieve from your child, a meal when you're sick—you put in a bid now, knowing that later you'll pay. You'll babysit for as long as you need to wipe out your debt. You won't skimp on meals you make for others. You'll open your house unforewarned at any time for an inspection to ensure that your services are valid. This past Christmas it was my friend Kathy's turn to host the Original Cookie Exchange's holiday gala. Kathy lives right across the street from me, and, for reasons that eluded me, I was formally invited.

I went wearing writer's black. Said goodnight to Jeremy and Bill, then stood on Kathy's stoop for a long undecided while before ringing the doorbell. From the sounds, one might have thought there was a construction site within—laughter sawed, high heels hammered, glasses clink-clinked, water ran. I leaned toward the nearest window to get a look, and there it all was in a riot: holly reds and greens, Santa sweaters, jingles on sleeves, muffy collars, battery-rigged candy canes lighting up pale ears. The Cookie Exchangers were squeezed into Kathy's galley kitchen, everything trip-wiring laughter. The dining room table was encrusted with trays of epicurean cookies, the sugar crystals catching the light like one of those faceted balls at a disco. The table's centerpiece was a bowl of acrylic-wrapped fortune cookies—my contribution, dropped off earlier in the day. *My cookie baking skills don't transcend the M&M variety*, I'd told Kathy, apologizing, as I handed over the box. She said the fortune cookies would be fine.

Once inside, I stood in the cloak of near invisibility and listened to the deluging gossip of those who knew each other well. No one story made any complete sense, but the strange small fragments were an intrigue, everything spiked with economic terms, everything a computation. *Remember when you did this for me because I had done that for you? Remember getting extra babysitting co-op points for simply changing a diaper? Remember when Susan took to her bed, and then Jane took to her bed, and we changed the rating system? I'm still in your debt. I've got plans for you. We've got to do something for Molly.* There was nothing sentimental about the business of this clan; what had to be done was efficiently done, and what was needed was asked for. Investments made for another were investments made for oneself, equal parts self-service and altruism. The circle of care was entirely equitable. There was always another hand to take the baton.

"You're here on behalf of Mary Anne," I heard Kathy tell me as the party started to jab out of the kitchen and squeeze toward the dining room. I looked down at the cookieless platter Kathy was thrusting my way, and then I moved, because her finger was pointing, to the place near the table that must have been reserved for Mary Anne. Every woman lined up then, as if at a Girl Scout meeting. There was a one-to-one correspondence between each Exchanger and each laden cookie tray; I, with my fortune cookie centerpiece and Mary Anne's plate, was the odd woman out. With a ceremonious clearing of throat, Kathy heralded the commencement of exchanging. "Ladies," she said, suppressing the smile she's always suppressing and shaking her short peachy hair, "the time is here. The time is now."

One by one, then, they started, each club member telling the story of the cookies she'd transported to the gala. Each story a ritual, cut from the same patterned cloth. If it was hard for the

Exchanger to leave her house for the party, that was where her cookie story started. If her Christmas tree had fallen down, or if she wanted a promise of prayers on account of a friend, or if she'd finally bought her husband the golf clubs he'd always wanted, that too was knitted into the preamble.

Subsequently the cookies themselves took center stage—the recipes, the odd ingredients, the kids stealing the dough, the husbands helping or not helping, the final, transportable yield. Relative difficulties of recipes were explained and noted—*I'm getting my master's, my husband is traveling, my father is dying, my little girl's reaching that stage.* Everything forgiven, understood, the stories presented above the laden table's menagerie of snowmen, rum balls, thumbprints, almond bars, gingermen with currant eyes. And when the stories were done, the cookie harvest began, each Exchanger moving in slow, patient sequence around the room, lifting precisely four cookies from each plate and arranging them, artistically, on her shiny take-home platter. Taking my cues from the crowd, I moved reverentially around the table, stopping at every cookie station, leaning in, daintily choosing four of each kind, putting them on the corners of the plate I had been inexplicably saddled with.

"Who's Mary Anne?" I asked Kathy when I was sufficiently out of earshot of the majority of Exchangers, when the *oohing* and the *aahing* had created a satisfactory hum.

"She's one of us," Kathy explained. "Only this year she couldn't come. She's home recovering from a double mastectomy."

"Oh," I said, taken aback, suddenly horrified at the prospect of failing to do her cookie plate justice.

"Yeah," Kathy said. "Mary Anne's got four kids. You better go around again and fill it up with extras."

For the longest time after the Exchange gala, I wondered why I'd been invited. I don't bake, after all, and I've never wangled a babysit trade, and anyone at all could have fixed a plate for Mary Anne. One day, still slightly bothered, I asked Kathy the question I'd been pondering. "I figured you should see how some of the rest of us do friendship," she answered. She went on to remark that she couldn't have survived without the co-op, and, knowing her situation as I do, I had to nod a gentle yes.

"I needed to get out, and I trusted these women, and never in ten years has any one of them forgotten to show up on time, and never once—and here I credit all the rules you roll your eyes at—have we had misunderstandings or falling-outs. We do what we promise to do and we never do more than anyone else, and every one of us has gotten through everything women—fate of the species—has to get through." Kathy was able to leave her young adopted son in good hands when her mother got cancer early on. When her son developed Tourette's, she once again knew she'd be okay—that she had a safety net, women who would help, that for the price of a regulated return favor, her child would get all the love Kathy has the wherewithal to give freely herself.

"But the cookies?" I asked, and Kathy admitted, yes, that was something extra, something that one of the members had concocted following two months spent lying pregnant in bed. "I thought at first that we were just suburban housewives gone real batty," Kathy said, remembering. "But then I realized that this was our chance to see each other without our kids. We used to get really dressed up for the night, our own rebellion against the scuzziness of our days.

"Nothing was ever said about having to bring in homemade cookies," she went on, "but after the first exchange, it was clear there were some very good cooks in the crowd, so we all quietly decided to try harder and harder recipes each year. We put the emphasis on presentation. We wanted to give each other cookies that no one in their right mind would take the time to bake. We wanted to pass around our recipes, report on snafus. The rest of the rituals just happened, I guess. But what can I say? The cookies are great, and so is our gang. Wherever I end up next, I'm going to be more open-minded to the ways people get together so it doesn't all seem like such a lonely voyage."

"Oh," I said, for she had given me much to think about.

"Yeah," said Kathy. "And that's what I wanted you to see for yourself."

I don't know where Julie went after that frantic rainstorm call. She left her job abruptly, and no one there could track her down. At her funky apartment no one answered the phone, and when I went to find her at her second-shift job, I was told that she was no longer reporting for work. I sent letters, didn't hear a word. I never, in all this time, have found out where Julie went, and I don't know about her brood, and it hits me hard every time I think of Lynn without "her Chulie"; Jason undone, alone; Robert losing the only person who ever calmed him down.

I was reading yesterday about the female octopus. How in her whole life she mates only once, then plants her thousands of eggs in a swilling grotto. The eggs in their place, she then ornaments the cave with garlands from the ocean's underworld. When she's done planting and decorating, her real work begins: she blows on her eggs, moving the water over the clusters, doing everything she can to keep those maybe babies strong. She blows so much that she has no time to eat. She blows herself into exhaustion; she won't sleep. Maybe one or two of the baby octopuses will make it. For her part, in the end she's all used up. She huddles down in her grotto when her babies squeeze out to life, and, with the hordes of unhatched eggs, she dies.

What would happen, you have to wonder, if the father octopus spelled the mother? Or if a community of mothers, Exchangers one and all, took turns dressing the watery cave and blowing on the eggs? What would happen if we understood, in full, life's circles, how a pair of hands must reach for a pair of hands, and how the reaching cannot ever really stop, and how that's friendship? Somebody should have given Julie her one small deserved thing. And if no one did, if no one could, there should have been more for this great giver, in the end, than a man asking, demanding, yet again wanting more, in a rain-soaked parking lot.

13

Perfect
Strangers

PRESSING MY EAR TO THE WIND, I try to put myself where
Andrée now is: on a foreign hill, among perfect strangers, her
hand cradling her husband's tumor, her mind measuring the distance between her future and her past. Slogging through the
days, I wait for news. Holding Bill longer at night, holding
Jeremy, I wait. In the early afternoon, I take walks, telegraphing
heart talk to Andrée: *I am thinking of you. I am praying.*

These days it is a fact—sound as mathematics—that steeping
oneself in another's sorrow is a privilege, a danger, a sorrow unto
itself. Who, I keep wondering, is taking care of Andrée? On
what mountain, in whose house, in what language does she
mourn? Where does she lodge her giant grief? I need to believe
that someone is there for her when Lynn, Donna, her mother,
cannot be. I telegraph another prayer: *May you find a friend. May
goodness find you.*

Waiting for news, I wade back through time, through photographs in an attic box. I am struck, as I leaf through, by the
gestures of friendship that lie preserved in plastic sleeves. The

hand on a shoulder. The splinting of a parrot's wing. The giggle of schoolgirls. The rope of flowers across a grave.

Friendship isn't all big gestures, ecstatic moments. It is also the littlest things, the humanity that happens between people when you find yourself way out of context and someone reaches out and pulls you in. Friendship is also what eludes Kodachrome. Like the secrets between a maid and a foreigner.

I hold in my hand photographs of Nicha. In most she is doing her shy and awkward best to pretend that I have not shown up with my camera. She wears a blue dress and a long pink apron, or a pink dress with a yellow apron, and her feet are either bare or clad in the spongy white shoes that Bill's mother brought her from the States. In one photograph Nicha is slicing scallions, her lips drawn back over her toothless gums. In another she is sitting down, her hands slack in her lap, her black hair loose in its bun, her posture nevertheless suggesting alertness. We'd been married three years before Bill took me home, to his mother's house and her husbandless friends, to his brothers, to Tiburcio, to Nicha, to a country besieged by war as much as by beauty. It was Nicha, the maid, who made me feel most welcome there. Nicha who recognized and broke through the vulnerability I was feeling.

We had been in Santa Tecla less than twenty-four hours when we had to start packing for a retreat to the estuary house, two hours south. The guerrillas had been bombing electrical towers, and skirmishes had been reported three miles away. The military was out in force, and curfews were interrupting the parties. There were whispers of a possible embassy attack, so it was decided: we would leave.

No one was in a panic—all of this seemed to be routine—but

efficiency was imperative, and everybody had a role in the get-ting-ready-to-go that seemed universally understood, except by me. Everyone had something to pack or write down, someone to call, everyone was speaking a wild, captious Spanish, packing flashlights and bug spray and maps. With no assignment to my name and Bill on call for special duties, I decided to slip out of the way. I slid up the white marble steps and across the white marble floor and planted myself in the kitchen. I found a stool and sat down. I was Nicha's audience as she went about her chores.

Even at sixty, the age Nicha must then have been, her shoul-ders were square and strong, her legs solid as posts. She knew what she had to do, and she did it. She filled one gigantic silver trunk with blankets, linens, towels, and plates; on top of all that, she laid her Sunday uniform. The second trunk she packed, meticulously, with food. Frozen tortillas that looked like pan-cakes, scratched plastic containers of diced tomatoes and onions, fresh beans and beef, plantains, milk, leftover chicken. Nicha went about her business in even, unhurried fashion, unaffected, so it seemed, by the news that the guerrillas were circling in. Every now and then she looked up at me, and I smiled unpersuasively back. Out of pity, I guess, she brought me a glass of coconut milk, its white color so thin it seemed al-most blue.

Later that same morning, crammed into the back of an over-freighted Jeep, I again found myself in Nicha's company. She had the window, and I was next to her, fending off the weight of the cooler and the trunk stacked on my right side. Bill was up front next to his mother and his two brothers, and behind us was a second car stuffed full of people and things. At some invisible signal, Bill's mother turned the key in the Jeep, and our caravan started to rumble. It was May, and the roads and earth were dry, and through the crack in the windows, shards of stone and dust flew. Nothing felt more oppressive than the Spanish, which rose and fell indecipherably all around me.

Only Nicha wasn't talking, and I took some comfort in that. I kept my eyes peeled on the country outside the car as we drove by open market stalls, where women sat dwarfed beside buckets of blue and purple flowers, buckets of crab, split fish, buckets of pounded corn. We drove by babies in boxes, in barrels, on a crush of ripe tomatoes; we drove by soldiers standing guard at every corner. We drove by earthquake shelters; by homes built out of rubble, cardboard, thatch; by the rotting carcasses of dead cattle; by a gang of raunchy cats. Rolled mats, hard earth, iron pots, bloated tummies blurred by as we drove, faster and faster.

The road grew straighter and wider as we left the town. Now the soldiers looked like wooden toys propped up on the margins of the road. Their rifles hung from their belts like a warning. Their backs were straight as pins. "What's going on?" I called up to the front of the car, but Bill, in the middle of another conversation, didn't hear. "What's going on?" I yelled this time; he answered briefly: I should relax. I should look around. This was beautiful country we were in, and I shouldn't worry: we were safe.

I turned to look at Nicha. She just kept staring straight ahead. I remembered what Bill had said about her: *She bore twelve children alone.* Bore them on the side of a jungle hill, cutting their cords herself with broken bottle necks. She did not have the features of a heroine. Her mouth, without its teeth, was gentle-looking, nearly concave. I turned my eyes back toward the highway and saw that the view was opening up to a flatter landscape. I saw women wearing jugs on their heads, a man leading an ox through a field. In the distance I perceived what appeared to be a kiln, a primitive thing like an igloo, its façade a lovely Tuscan red. Smoke leaked from a hole in its top. Despite the cloying perspiration, I leaned across Nicha to get a better look. She turned to see what I was looking at, and, in that instant, made a brick shape with her hands. She tapped at the window and made the brick shape again, and I nodded and smiled to say I understood. To say thank you for explaining the kiln.

Who in South Korea is explaining things to Andrée? I keep wondering this, even as I wait here and remember. Even though I know that friendship could happen to her in a foreign place.

After we had driven between cotton fields and across a volcanic ridge, after we'd slowed, with the traffic, into a single lane, then sped back up, then slowed again, the car Nora was driving veered off the asphalt onto a gouged-out, unpaved path. Now there were fat, peeling trees and wild turkeys on either side of us, men in Panama hats, children who wore nothing but wooden crosses at their necks. At the end of the road, at the edge of the sea, Bill's mother parked her Jeep and pointed straight ahead. There was a *lancha*, waiting in the mangroves, our final transport to the estuary. There were the men who were to navigate the waters, having some smokes in the shade.

It was high tide, and that meant taking off our shoes, scrunching up our clothes, and wading out to where the thatch-roofed ferry was docked. Black pigs and a stray dog had beaten us to the shore. We walked between them, boarded, and waited while Nicha went back and forth through the muck, transporting the trunks and supplies. Two huge ovals of sweat marked the armpits of her dress when at last she was able to join us. I sat at one end of the *lancha*, and Nicha, facing me, tipped the weight at the other end. Between us sat Bill, his family, his friends, and the rising wave of yet another conversation. *What are you talking about?* I almost leaned over to ask him, but the talk started breaking hilariously, like whitecaps. In English Bill speaks with quiet, careful rhythms. In Spanish he is hands, face, body, an unfamiliar, helpless laughter. Spanish is home, and I knew that no matter what I thought to ask him then, there would be no explaining it.

We reached the estuary house at three P.M., when the sun was still a blight in the sky. I carried what I could from the *lancha* into the house, while Nicha set to work stocking the kitchen, making the beds, busting cobwebs, beating the dust out of the hammocks that hung between palm trees outside. The house, cinderblock, sturdy, sat right on the beach. There were mosquitoes; Nicha lit citronella. She aired out smells, shook out curtains, got water moving through the faucets. When she was done, the others stretched out in their hammocks. I wasn't going to sleep. I took a walk.

I want to show you the pictures I took that day. The faces of La Barra de Santiago. I want to take you down those roads of poverty and bougainvillea so that you can see the colors as I saw them—the brilliant orange lilies and the snapping lemon roses and the crimson leaf that a girl waved at me as if it were some kind of flag. The estuary had been invaded by Caucasians, it was clear, for all the children there were of mixed heritage. They had black Latin hair and aqua eyes, or huge chocolate Jeremy eyes and corn-colored halos on their heads. They wore filthy, torn First Communion dresses; they wore American tee shirts; they wore nothing at all. Their houses were bamboo and thatch or long swatches of fabric, and the place was silent—an eerie silence—as if words had never made it there at all. The estuary kids climbed out of buckets, crawled out from the bamboo, slid beneath barbed wire, stood on guard before a solid turquoise fence and stared at the camera I was holding. I found a boy stuck up high in a tree. His feet were long, his legs were skinny. He could have been five. He could have been fifteen.

I walked that estuary until the sun went from a hot white sphere in the sky to a diffuse golden color. I walked until I understood that I would never understand the mysteries that had shaped my husband, the wild synapses of color, impoverishment, light that formed his expectations of this world and defined his bridges to it. I walked until a murmur broke the silence and the murmur wasn't birds but a dozen Salvadorans in hammocks strung up in the trees. The place was dense with the smell of citronella. A funnel of iridescent smoke escaped a chimney. I could hear water slapping against the beach, the song of a guacalchia in the trees, the arcing, dangling, jittery talk of Bill's mother, his brothers, his friends. I could hear Bill laughing, at ease, Bill finally home, full of Spanish. I circled the house and looked for Nicha.

She was clearing away used plates when I found her, leaving them to soak in a tub of water. It was clear that there had been some kind of late afternoon party, and she had not heard me enter, did not know I was there. With her back to me, she started eating a taco, gumming it down hungrily. She ate like a prisoner, fast and greedy. She wiped her mouth with the back of her hand.

"Nicha," I addressed her by name for the very first time, speaking as softly as I could. "Nicha," I repeated. "Hola."

Startled, she turned, an expression of guilt on her face. When she saw me, she blushed and clumsily smiled, then closed her lips quick, over her gums. She swiped again at her mouth with the back of her hand and visibly tried to decide what to do. I motioned that she should finish her meal. I stepped back to give her some room. But Nicha must have misread my hands; she thought I was asking for supper. I tried to gesture again, but she put her taco aside, and soon there was no going back. Container by container, Nicha started delidding Tupperware. She retrieved a plate from the suds and rinsed it clean. When she finally got around to making the taco, she gave it every ounce of extra care. She rolled the tomatoes into the onions, and into this she rolled the meat, and when she was finished, she passed the taco to me. I had no choice but to accept what she offered. I stood beside her in that kitchen, the drool of meat sauce on our chins.

Out in the hammocks the Spanish was muted. The moon was rising over the bay. The next day guerrillas would shell the U.S. embassy, and government soldiers would open fire, and the news would come through on the transistor radio. These are the details that no one then told me. These are the details I would read about later, in American papers, when I got back home.

I loved Bill more and knew him less after that trip to his country. But I went back a handful of times, knowing that Nicha's goodness would find me, knowing and trusting in the sacrament of small gestures, the capacity of perfect strangers to put one's mind at rest. It's all I want for Andrée now. A mug of tea. An opened door. A freshened pillow for her head. A friendship in a foreign place in the face of so much danger.

14

From Silence
Grows

ONE DAY LAST WINTER, Jeremy and I were feverbound in the middle of a snowstorm. In my arms he lay, glowing like a fragile ember, seeing stars blink, he vaguely mentioned, on our bare white ceiling. I was telling him stories or letting him be or bringing him cherry Popsicles to help douse the flames. There was no one around but us and the silence, the weather having wrapped the house like some giant steel-gray muffler. The clock seemed full of regrets, unwilling to give up the hour, and the clouds held their own against the sun; there was no ray, no glisten. There was nothing much that could be done, and so we lay there, waited.

All day long the phone didn't ring. All day long the fever teased, then came back stronger. I was privately fighting doubts about the work I was supposed to be doing, the book I was supposed to be writing. By four o'clock we lay in shadows. By five it was black outside, no light anywhere beyond our windows. We had set ourselves up in the living room by then. I'd drawn a light sheet up to Jeremy's shoulders, and his head was in my lap. I was stroking his damp, dark, endlessly soft silky hair, listening to the sound of his breathing.

Faintly then, faintly, I heard a sound like someone chewing ice cubes. Big boots, it seemed, breaking through the virgin snow. Crunching they came, then something hurtled through the air. A slam. A stumble. The big boots went away. "Did you hear that?" I whispered to Jeremy, when the silence whooshed back in. "Maybe," he whispered back, and closed his eyes. "Maybe I did. It could be something."

With a nurse's care I shifted Jeremy on the couch, rearranged his cotton sheet, and slipped out to the door. A gust of cold smacked me hard, high, in the face; a twizzle of tears fell from my eyes. I switched on the porch light and squinted after the footprints, then found the manila envelope that had been delivered. "What's this?" I asked no one, for the boots were long gone. Bending down toward the drifted snow, I recognized the stylish writing: Kate, from San Francisco. In the frigid, unforgiving air I broke the envelope's seal and found a book about friendship. A sheet of loose paper floated out from the book's pages. *Thought you might be needing this. I believe in what you're doing, Beth. Don't lose faith in yourself. Just keep going.*

Maybe I have not said enough about the cosmic stuff of friendship, the gifts that arrive in the snow. I have not taken you with me on my walks with Joanne, sung the sound of the laughter that threw us to the curb, even though we weren't even talking. I have not described for you the royal red velvet jewelry bag that Bambi slipped like a secret into my house, nearly unnoticed, or the night Tom drove me down to the shore so that I — alone, apart from him — could pitch broken clam shells into the surf and heal an anger. I haven't mentioned what it was like, some months ago, to rediscover JC and Jane. Their family of five, our family of three, in the back of an old-fashioned diner. Their Johnny and our Jeremy performing magic tricks and the lamest jokes, their Claire and their Alice nibbling, giggling, Jane remembering that trunk of towels she hauled on behalf of my marriage, JC recalling the battle of scumbags back when architecture mattered, all of us doubled up over practically nothing, weeping calamitously over absolute nonsense, in a raunchy, greasy diner. Maybe the effects of friendship must finally go uncharted. Maybe there is always wonder, after all. How did Kate know what I was missing that day? Whose boots were they in the snow? How many times does a chasm of nothing yield the gift you didn't know you were needing?

I have wanted to teach Jeremy about friendship, but, inevitably, he has taught me too. About the holiness of simply sitting, waiting. About the companionable qualities of silence.

Forty-eight hours after his fever broke, on a day of frozen rain and smothering snow, we sat at the table across from each other, I watching his face: God's greatest miracle. I had gotten the fever that finally danced away from him, and was slowed to the drear of the day. Jeremy sat, his eyes lit like the phosphorescent scales of fish, in perfect, congenial quiet.

We knew, because we had peered out the windows of every downstairs room, that we would be going nowhere that day. The glass-topped table on the deck was hung with a bright fringe of ice. The bushes along the back were entombed, and the pine had keeled spectacularly to the ground, like a long-haired cat arching its back. The tall, multibranching horse chestnuts, maples, white birches, and oaks wore sheer castings of ice that split, just like that, and smashed fantastically to the ground; the ice from the telephone wires clung, fell, joined the crystal smatterings that twinkled the ground, the pavement, the road: a perilous place. Only salting trucks were driving by.

In the house, beads of heat-seeking moisture had pooled their resources and been transformed into a drip: a discordance in a newly painted room. A miniature Niagara was cleansing the dusty basement steps, and above my head the ceiling was turning the brown of a Bartlett pear gone bad. The house was no longer weather-tight, but, again, we had no place to go.

So we sat. Jeremy finished the soup that came from a can because I hadn't cooked, and I finished my yogurt. A tower of laundry rose like foam to my right. There was a big mess of bills on the floor. I could have dealt with either of the piles, or sopped the water from the ceiling, or chipped the ice away from the dangerously slicked front stoop, or talked to my son. But there was something more entrancing to be had right then. Silence was coursing through the miscreant water. There was Jeremy's face—skin the color of cream, eyes black as purple, one eyebrow slightly higher than the other. Muscles shimmied beneath the pinpricks of his freckles. I could tell by the tilt of his expression that he was whorled up into soccer again. He was having, as he says, a thought.

It was Technicolor. As big and mesmerizing as a planetarium. Seated front and center before his own imagination, Jeremy appeared to have lost consciousness of the ice outside or the hollow, metallic drumming of the leaks dripping into cups and bowls. He was in a dome, and the sky above the dome was blue, and there wasn't a spare seat in the house. Barcelona and Atletico Madrid had taken the field. The coaches were on the sidelines, pacing. A whistle was blown, a startling ping I read from the tremble in my son's lips. Tensing forward in the floral upholstery of the dining room chair, Jeremy directed his attention to a still-dry point where the kitchen walls T-ed into the ceiling. The ball was put into play on the field, and Jeremy smelled it, heard it, his cheeks flushed pink. Something tugged at one corner of his mouth, his nose crinkled, his eyes stared brave, then blinked hard, and then his face crumpled in upon itself and he slumped back into the garden of his chair. Someone had missed a goal, I supposed. It was a lost opportunity, and Jeremy knew it.

I should have gotten to the bills or to the soft knot of laundry, thrown more towels at the sick, ripe stain that festered and widened above my head. I should have, could have talked. But water oozed and time stayed still. Jeremy threw his arms up in a V. *Score!*

"Whoa," he said. "Mom. That was a heel kick."

"No way," I said.

"It's true," he said.

And then there was the silence, again.

Teaching a child the noisy nature of friendship is nothing like being taught what silence is. There is a silence that is loss, aloneness, death, the irreconcilable. And there is a silence that is the obverse. I remember climbing the steps to my grandmother's room when I was nine. She was dying. It was the end.

"Grandmom," I would call to her beneath the steep ascent of stairs. "Grandmom." A whisper on every step. It was a child's way of gifting time, for I knew that in the long pause of the stair she would disguise the basin by her knees, pull the sheets across her legs, and press a sterling silver brush to her head, where a few black, coarse hairs still ribboned through the soft, thin dandelion puffs. I knew that she would rub her cheeks to bring the blood back up. That she would grow as upright and tall as she still could in that wide, white, window-facing bed.

When she had done what she could, she would call to me with a name that was ours alone. She would reach for me when I crossed the threshold of her room and came toward her bed, and she would empty her fingers into mine, as if to forestall their flight. But she was not afraid; this I know. She was confident to the end that sixty years were not standing between us; that pain is simply suffered; that life, even in its rawest form, is good.

The last time it was August hot. The last time I came too soon. She was without her dressing—lying there in the white sheets like Braille, so small, so white in her white bed, not a book, not a magazine nearby, her eyes on the window, her painted jewelry box the lonely color in that room. I remember staring at her from the threshold, then taking off my shoes. Running down the hall and down the steps. Turning at the bottom stair, now calling her name, loudly, defiantly. "Grandmom," I called from the second stair. "Grandmom," from the third. Calling "Grandmom, Grandmom," all the way up, through the stale, oppressed, hot August air, until I heard my name called back from that room. That day I sat on the edge of Grandmom's bed and said nothing at all. She was watching the window, and I watched it with her. We had the silence to ourselves.

I am here. You are here. We are, in this shaft of sun, in this blink of time, in this foreverness and neverness, together. It is more than can be said with words.

. . .

At the kitchen table Jeremy was laughing about half-time. About the locker-room goings-on that he could see, hear, smell, believe. How great is that, to have a whole live-play action in your brain? To be able to sit peaceably while the porous house drips weather, to be entertained and gratified by your own effulgent mind?

And how great is it—how really astonishing and stunning— to sit in front of him, imagining his imagination? Two yellow cards. An illicit slide tackle. A second goal. Wild celebration. The fans going crazy in the stands. I sat watching in the gray, damp, dripping silence, just reading the page of his face—the O's of his eyes, the typography of his eyebrows, the twinge of deepening commas at his nose's bridge. Once in a while he attached a phrase to what he could see, descended from wherever he was for a report. "The marking is awful," he'd tell me. Or "There's a hat trick in sight." "The corner kick got headed in; the keeper just couldn't make the play."

"That was something else," I'd say, keeping my hand on my chin so I wouldn't reach across the sticky soup bowl and stroke his temple. "I can't believe the score's two-nil."

"It's a really good game," he opined, his eyes still on the kitchen ceiling, his smile nothing short of holy. "One of the best I've seen in a long time."

Mutually agreeable silence is an earned luxury, the ultimate measure, perhaps, of a bond. You learn that in family. You also learn it in friendship—I learned it when we flew to Paris to see Anne and her children and Jean-Yves, Anne's gentle husband, who opened their house to us for two long well-lit days—the romance of the Musée d'Orsay, Notre-Dame, and the Latin Quarter mere train track miles away.

I wasn't sure it would work out. Didn't know what we'd have to say to one another—we the foreigners now, they the natives. Anne had lost some of her English since moving back home, and her kids, two lovely puckery-cheeked elves, tinkled on endlessly in French. Their house was all white, inside and out. Tall and tiled, impeccably modern, nothing at all like the house they had occupied in our neighborhood of tiny, elderly homes.

But there were alluring hints of the familiar, such as the way Anne set her salmon pastries and chocolate pears upon the plates. The way Jean-Yves poured the drinks, the way the kids dragged their stuffed animals and broken books from floor to floor, looking for a shelter for their tea party. We weren't there for five minutes before the little ones were off with Jeremy, before Bill and I had taken our chairs in Anne and Jean-Yves's generous kitchen. Jean-Yves began to speak of his travels; Bill remembered some of his. Anne told of a case she'd argued in court; I spoke of books I had discovered that season. We talked about the kids, about the city. We talked about social justice and politics, about the deaths of famous people, about old trees. Anne looked for words and Jean-Yves helped her find them, and after dessert we turned the pages of their many photo albums, spoke of holidays, baptisms, friends. I signed their guest book. Anne spoke of her parents, Jean-Yves told stories. We retired to our rooms when the moon was high. The next morning, at breakfast, the house was exceptional, still. There was bread in the baskets and coffee in the mugs, and Bill and Jeremy and I were welcomed into our hosts' daybreak rituals. We were invited to sit in the pool of audacious morning light and be there with them, no talk required. They made us feel as if we belonged, and in that sunlight, in that lovely quietude, our friendship deepened, settled, held us.

15

Correspondence

Dear Beth:

have you ever seen an echocardiogram? today, i watched a moving black-and-white picture of my husband's heart, the flap thrashing vigorously, almost violently, as if it had a mind of its own. it never struck me before: every machine is moved by some engine, but where is the engine that keeps the heart going? think about it. later the news that the cancer has invaded his heart, and that his heart will stop its beating in three weeks' time. my husband is very brave, i think. we are still praying for miracles, of course.

   with love,

Beth—

i met a woman wandering the halls of the cancer ward with me. about my mother's age. she lost her husband to cancer at age 48, a daughter to same at age 34, and here she is watching her remaining daughter, age 40, battle her cancer. she almost re-married at age 50, she said, but her fiance died on the operating table. on monday her car was parked next to the porsche that caught on fire in the hospital parking garage, bringing every firetruck in town. her name is Jenny. she told me she's praying for my husband.

    love,

Dear Beth,
there's a winnie the pooh postcard i saw that goes, "i just wanted to be sure of you". so i steal this minute from someone else to be sure of you, you whom i have neglected and whose caring emails i pile up. if there is anything beautiful about death i don't see it; it's dragging of heels all the way. what there is, though, is grace enough for the day, and one answer to one prayer, at least: time to love my husband. time for him to know.

    are you well?

Beth:
Jesus said, "mourn with those who mourn, rejoice with those who rejoice". empathy IS something. i will keep you posted, of course.

beth:
if it would damage our friendship to not talk, i will talk. otherwise please bear with me for now. nothing is certain. you have stood by me in my trials in this subjective state of mind, and it seems to me that's the criterion of friendship.

    love, andrée

16

FAITH

IT IS NOT YET SPRING and I long for birdsong. I long for a leaf on a tree, for the purple of a crocus, for the wind to stop blowing so hard. There is one room in this house that the sun oozes into. I've laid a box of memories under its spell.

I have pulled a chair into the sunlight, and now I sit in this trapezoid of mullioned yellow, fractions of the past on my lap. Letters, mostly, and every once in a while a bit of ribbon, a flattened paper bow. I move most slowly through these things, afraid of loosening the atoms, converting history to dust. A plane flies a straight line over my head, then all is dormant once more.

What falls out into the mild sun is a bud, the relic of a striped carnation that has been crisped and puckered by time. I hold it flat in my palm, noticing how the pin that spears its stem gleams in the mute daylight. The concoction of petals looks like the hem of a Victorian dress. The white has faded to a sepia brown, the red is the color of dried blood. I try to think what occasion this bud is from, why I might have wanted to preserve it.

The answer eludes me. I do not remember this crushed carnation. I lay it down on the shelf near where I'm sitting, and into
that hollow in the chair where so many heads have fit before, I
rest my own. I close my eyes and try to conjure a world without
the spectacle of flowers. The earth as it was one hundred million
years ago. Soggy. Green. Not a dahlia, lily, or apple blossom in
sight. No acacia or goldenrod or rebellious blade of grass. We
had not yet swung out of the trees, and there wasn't a single
feminine heart that could be ripened with desire. Angiosperm,
the word, means "encased seed." Angiosperm, the invention,
yielded pineapples, berries, almonds, honeysuckle—it is a
smack of energy in a nifty concentrate form. Loren Eisley said it
best: "The appearance of the flowers contained also the equally
mystifying emergence of man." So, like it or not, flowers made
us.

The room in which I sit is characterized by sparseness. It's the
way I like to arrange my space: air and light sovereign over objects. In the length of one paragraph, I can name every article in
this room: my husband's guitar; Macaroni, the stuffed clown;
the polished-to-walnut high-top shoes that carried my father's
first toddler steps. A simple wooden rocker, a puppet carried
home from Prague, pictures in frames, two lamps, an antique
wool wheel whose great, flat circumference is hammered un-
evenly into place with wooden nails. One wall is books. One
wall is glass. There are a chair and a loveseat and a throw rug.
And above the broken radiator, on the far side of the room, sits
a waxy, imperiled plant. It holds the promise of an orchid, but
nothing blooms.

Ten months ago I had a party—invited every friend I thought
I had, cleared the downstairs of its occasional furniture, opened

the kitchen to the culinary talents of my mother and a caterer. I wanted my friends together, all at one time, all in one place, as real people, not as words, and I planned the Big Event for months. Rehabbing the downstairs bathroom, refreshing the baseboards, snatching the weeds out of the garden, rinsing the crud from the vases, painting the concrete pad at the door a forest shade of green. What was I celebrating? My marriage. Our child. People I admire. A book I wrote. I was celebrating June and coatless weather, the triumph of being alive. I wanted to gather my friends in one place and hold them, like a portrait, for a while. I wanted Jeremy to see the house filled like this.

The point is this. The day came, and our tiny Tudor-style house filled not just with people but with flowers. The vases I'd washed were hurriedly pressed into service, then water pitchers took their turn, and then the tall drinking glasses were deployed and, in one reckless case, a bucket. After twenty minutes or so my sublime friend Jamie, whose own arrangement had arrived primped up in a basket, took the lead—bargaining for sink time with the caterer, scissoring stem tips, combining bouquets, whispering status reports in my ear. The four downstairs rooms were suddenly transformed by fragile colors, and the flowers kept coming—tucked in friends' arms like so many infants, rescued by Jamie, propped upright, marched into one room or the other for display. That day I felt wealthier than a person has a right to feel. I felt permeable, entered into, by a sustaining fellowship.

Next morning the downstairs was still missing most of its furniture. The rooms had the feel and the smell of a garden; sun crept in. I walked from vase to vase taking pictures; studying freesia, lavender, calla lily, iris; putting a name to each arrangement. Jean and Ann, the yellow, blue, and white. Christine, the

abundant scarlet. Karen, the reds and greens. Mary Beth and
Felicity, the gorgeous, tenuous pink. Ellen, the purple, my
neighbor Joan, the midnight blues. I lined the vases up on the
windowsills, on the floor, on the battered wood cover that hides
the useless radiator, and I stood between them and among them,
knowing that they would fade. The petals would singe with age,
the stems would slump, the leaves would crape and crinkle, and
the water they were sipping would turn an algae green. Flowers
are an illusion. Flowers are transcendent. A week later I was out
in my back yard putting the dead stems to rest. They decom-
posed over the course of that summer, and by September they
were gone.

What remained, after the week of flowers, was the orchid,
along with the stone called FAITH, both of which had been delivered by Amy. She had winged in from the land of San Francisco just for my party, had spent the Party Eve sleeping on a
couch downstairs, and then, on Party Day, had disappeared.
When she returned she was staggering beneath the weight of
the stone and the phalaenopsis. The name doesn't do the plant
justice.

Have you ever really looked at the gymnastics of an orchid?
When Amy found me in the hallway that day, this is what surprised me first: the outrageous bends and nips and turns of the
shivering blooms she was holding, the defiant bridge between
stalk and bloom, the dangling participle of beauty. Next came
the thought that has plagued me since: *I'll never do right by this
orchid.* I'm the woman, after all, who can't keep phlox in bloom,
the one with weeds that whorl around my mailbox. My tiger
lilies die spectacular, fiery deaths. My mums are strangled by ivy.
I planted six dozen forget-me-nots early last May and never saw
a speck of blue.

But there Amy was with this sculpture of orchid blooms and her fist opening to FAITH. Some things I run from, but not Amy's enthusiasms, so I accepted the orchid and made it a centerpiece, along with the heart-shaped sugar cookies and my mother's savory bread. The next day I moved it to my study, and a few weeks later I paraded it straight to the bathroom. The room was newly rehabbed, after all, and I believed that its pleasant humidity would make the big plant feel at home, as if it had landed in a rain forest.

Now the orchid is here in this room, where I've been sitting all this time, musing about friendship and flowers. I am hoping that a change of view will do it good.

Easing back into the chair, I'm suddenly inundated with memories of rooms filled with friends. My mother has always been especially good at binding her friends into the pages of a party, everyone chaptered together with poached salmon and pasta, my grandmother's meat sauce, fizzy punch, a clown, a portrait artist, a piano player. Likewise my friend Mary Beth, whose home is the site of one near-continuous party, all of us circulating in and out, always a cobbler in the oven, Jean at the sink, Felicity in charge of restocking toilet paper, somebody pitching toys, dog bones, rags down the basement steps, Deb arranging the plates on the buffet. Mary Beth's parties have themes: Halloween, soccer, a book we've all been told to read. We have all gotten to know one another, so Mary Beth's friends are now also my friends, an enlargement of my circle. The same holds true when I go to Jamie's house, her friends becoming my friends over broiled chicken and gazpacho, people I ask about later when Jamie and I are on the phone. *How's Bob? How's Debbie? Will you do me a favor and ask him to please pop that girl the question?* And then there's Lori and her spectacular home—her little girl, Meredith, collecting our coats, her husband filling our glasses.

In the grand red-brick Victorian on the multiethnic fringe of Philadelphia, where David and Kristin and their big dog Truman live, such melding of communities happens seasonally. David and Kristin's entourage go there to sample whatever gourmet dish Kristin has concocted, exchange news about foreign encounters, watch each other's kids get another season older. We stand in their spirited urban garden or, like risen water, around the staircase or on the canvas painting that is their kitchen floor, varnished enough, they reassure us, to withstand the abuse of our feet.

Parties are an illusion, everything transformed and crooked, lovely and staunch in its crookedness, tripping toward a delectable danger. Stories told like performances, conversation catapulting from guest to guest, elbows and smiles held at severe cranks and angles, which in private conversation are hardly necessary. At every party someone stands in the center looking out, one part of her brain buzzing: *This is the who of my life.* Even for children, parties seal something in wax: the idea of oneself as revealed by the faces in the corners, on the sofas, at the buffet, on the front stoop.

There is something to putting the people you know or want to know all in one place at one time, gathering them there, in the noise, like material objects—proof positive that you're alive, one of us all. As I grow older, I give more parties—set aside a day and write everybody I know a card and tell them to come for no reason: *Come as you are.* When they're here, I turn on the music and pass the plates and let myself be here with them. Then, when they're gone, I mingle with their ghosts, or handle the flowers they've deposited, or lean toward the echo of their chatter.

When you're a child, your friends are how you spend your time. When you're a teen, they help define you, dispel your only-ness. When you're grown up, they bring you news of the finiteness of things; they bring you flowers. They bring you back to your own memories by unveiling some of theirs, they make aging all right, make it the journey you're sharing. Friendship, at a certain point, becomes the stuff of narrative. It becomes character and plot, the effluvium of your house, long after the party is over.

It's been seven months since Amy's orchid has been anything but stem and leaves. The last flower it had lost its instincts first, and then the puff in its cheeks, and then the green arch that had bridged it to its stalk. It looked like a withered honeysuckle in the end. There was nothing to be gained by pressing it, for posterity, within a clump of letters.

I have watered this orchid religiously since it was transferred from Amy's hands to mine. I have paid it regular attention every day. I have gone up the street and asked the nursery for a tip sheet, and then I have pored over the Xeroxed pages, opening my mind up to instructions. *Best in east or southeast windows,* the tip sheets say. *Never allow to go bone dry. Spray it for mites. Fertilize with a blossom booster.* Take care.

Plants have active roots and cells, stomata, veins. Plants have food factories and sex, attitudes, needs, the desire to keep themselves alive. Last year's party has come and gone. The furniture is back in place. My friends have all scattered, and memories are flooding me. I'm no good with gardens, and this winter has brought sadness, and I can't remember to whom this striped carnation ever belonged. But Amy's orchid is still green, and I have time to boost it into bloom. I'll have another party in a few months, and another next year, and another, for as long as I'm standing. Illusion or no illusion, alchemy or truth, I like the sound of all that clatter. I like the cockle and the aftermath. The stone called FAITH, and the buds my friends, in their infinite wisdom, think to leave behind.

17

Passing
Away

WHEN HE PASSES AWAY the only thing you can hear is the heat, unseasonably strong. Andrée leaves a message. I return the call. "He died," she whispers, "and he was at home, in our bed. My heart beats too fast. My lungs feel crushed in. I cannot catch my breath. All I ever wanted was one more day with him. One more day. And now he's gone."

The next day is Sunday, Memorial Day weekend. There's a blessedly small showing in my third-grade Sunday school class. For the first time all year, the room doesn't echo with too many voices, and there's enough space around the table for me to sit down too. We read from the Book of Acts about Dorcas, a woman of good works, a seamstress. Dorcas has died, and the widows, her friends, are milling about, weeping, showing Peter the disciple her handiwork, insisting that she should have lived, because she did good works. Studying the woman, her garments, her friends, Peter raises his hand and with that gesture lifts Dorcas up. She is restored to the band of the living.

"Can that really happen?" Jeremy asks, his eyes two illuminated circles, and Laura says, "Yes, because it happened to Jesus." Danny just shakes his head back and forth, unwilling to make a commitment.

After church, Jeremy and I go to the only fine jewelry store that is open on Sunday. After considering everything the earnest saleslady shows us, we settle on a Russian Fabergé egg—a frosted oval pendant with a scarlet cross enameled on its face. We wait until the clerk has wrapped it in bone-colored ribbons, and then I take Jeremy home. Kissing my husband and son goodbye, I'm off again, driving to the old neighborhood, no scarf for my head this time, no plan but to sit wherever Andrée is sitting and listen to whatever she says.

I expect a prayerlike pall. Instead, I find the two youngest kids watching cartoons and Andrée behind a closed door in the back room. The little girl unlatches the screen door for me, and I'm suddenly overcome with a surge of motherly fondness as she lets me in, takes my hand, and calls out, "Mom, it's your friend for you coming." The door of the back room cracks open, and the palest possible version of Andrée slips through; her milk-colored jeans stop right below her knees, her feet are bare, her face and hair have hardly any color. "I'm sorry," I tell her over the din of the TV, taking her into my arms. "I'm sorry. I'm sorry. I'm sorry." Then we unclasp and sit in the room with the kids—she against one wall, I against the other. The phone keeps ringing. People come and go. Who knows where the older children are.

The memorial service is a week and two long days later. The weather now is a toxin, with the newscasts warning against straying outside, the houses insulated with the rattling disquiet of air conditioners and fans. I spend most of the day in my husband's cavelike basement, which is so much cooler than the swamp of the house. In this damp subterranean space, I am acutely aware of Bill's presence in all things hung, hidden, waiting. The piece of wood banged into the cinderblock with its bracelet of eight long rusted nails. The sepia-toned photographs of our son. His paintings and plaster casts, bottles of ink, rubber eyedroppers, measures and rules, templates, strings, squeezed-hard tubes of oil paint, the easel he has no time to use. And in the niches, on counters and shelves, the replica of a human skull, old cornsilks, dried lilac, bugs in jars. On one wall, taloned on with four stripes of masking tape, a watercolor of a man in a thin sienna-ocher shed. On a shelf, the basswood model of the desk Bill would love to build, very Japanese, pure, light as a single sheet of paper on the palm of my hand. In another corner, the heavy books on their precarious shelves, which Bill studies at night, sitting alone in the chair I've borrowed, listening to the groans of the earth. The ceiling is unfinished rafters and snaking copper pipes, and woven within, like the stretchy potholders children make, are wooden rods, planks, materials for projects not yet begun. No one ever finishes his life. Nothing is ever complete. Our souls are in the things we love and the ways we arrange them.

The memorial service is packed. Long before the music starts, the seminary auditorium is overflowing. I have arrived early, and I'm sitting far to the back, watching the room fill up. In the front row of this vast academic theater sit Andrée and, in ascending order of their ages, the children her husband has left behind. The older boy and girl, with whom I once shared finches and friendship, are appallingly grown up, immune to my presence. The girl, her wrist tattooed, wears skintight, high-split lycra; when she moves I see the paprika still flashing in her hair. The boy, exotically handsome, wears a respectful, shiny vest and crisp white shirt, and he's helped his hair to black again, having spent most of the winter as a blond. The littlest girl is in a gay party mood, a butterfly of energy, while the nine-year-old boy sits staring straight ahead. It is he who shared his father's passion for Korean culture, who drew Korean symbols at the kitchen table, watched Korean movies, tagged along with his dad when his dad would have him, perfected the art of spelling his Korean name with a soft paintbrush. His loss is the most tragic, and he is sitting painfully still, two seats down from An-drée, who is closed in on her right by the pragmatic, loving Lynn. Unflagging in her good counsel and friendship, Lynn will keep Andrée strong throughout the service.

In their glamorous black suits and solid-colored ties, in their neat linen dresses and careful charcoal hair, the Koreans are out in force for the occasion. Ministers, classmates, students, busi-nessmen, writers, friends of the deceased, they assemble silently in one overspilling cluster. There will be no seats to spare, for through the two double-doored entrances, Andrée's community of friends and neighbors continue to come — husbands and wives in understated cotton clothing, trios of girlfriends, pairs of old men, teenagers, toddlers. Every woman who has stood by Andrée's side is here, and out in the hallway, where a reception is planned, at least half a dozen more are arranging lemon bars and brownies, grapes, cheese — five contiguous cardboard tables' worth of memorial service food. I find myself flanked by two Korean families, and behind me now is a large man with a tufted beard whose voice, it turns out, is a sweet wonder. When we sing the hymns, I secretly sing with him, harmonizing with all the other mourners, as I once sang in church with my dad. Before us all, staring down from the stage, are two large blankets of flowers, and a vase of three dozen blood-red roses.

There are prayers and songs, and now the part of the service in which we are asked to remember and share the first thing that comes to mind about the man who isn't here. *How does he appear to you when you close your eyes*, the minister inquires of the mourners. *I ask you now to take your time; nobody's rushing anywhere this evening.* In measured good time, the rememberers and storytellers head for the stage—sidling out of their plush auditorium seats, managing the pitch of the theater stairs, fiddling with the mike until it answers their height. My eyes locked on Andrée, her kids, the indomitable Lynn, I manage to remember nothing about the man who once lived next door.

Conflicting stories are told, impossible contradictions, every recollection a counterpoint to the previous story, the next story, so that there is no apparent reconciliation of the man with the man. He is what his friends make of him, what his friends have always made of him, who his friends, with their own chemistries and spark points, enabled him to be; that is what friendships do to and for us. He is the composite of the impressions he has left, the memories he made; he lies at the center of his friends. He is the man of spy novels, the man of the Bible, the patient counselor, the radical student, the dreamer, the realist, the husband, the sinner, the pop-culture critic, the historian, best friend of ministers, best friend of common gangsters. It's as if someone were slowly rotating a prism so that each face singly catches the light, while trapped within, where no one can see it, is the absolute truth of Andrée's husband. From where I'm sitting, I watch

Andrée receive the stories, many told in a struggle of English by men who until nine days ago spoke with her husband exclusively in Korean.

There are more songs afterward, beautiful songs. Seven Korean pastors form a scalloped edge around the mike and, with an elegant woman at the piano behind them, sing what has to be the gentlest hymn in all the world. A hymn of vowels sung in seven parts, an appeal or a petition or a promise offered on the dead man's behalf, loud enough for him to hear, wherever he is, however dust turning to dust captures sound waves. I don't understand a word, yet I know that a truth somehow is being found, some invincibility in the face of death, a sung command that every disparate strand of the disappeared man be kept in the thrumming hearts of his friends.

Driving home, the windows open, I feel the heat dragging itself out of the sky. Every now and then a cool, dark breeze darts its way through my hair, against my neck, into the white flesh of my eye. *How does he appear to you?* I hear the minister ask, and my mind unlocks its secret gates and lets me in to a buried image of Andrée's husband. It is the last day I saw him alive, one month before anyone suspected the cancer lurking in his lungs, when he still had dreams of writing a novel, of finishing his history, of growing old with his family and friends. In an Annapolis storefront I had found something for Andrée—a mirrored silver cross made in the heartland of Mexico—and with Bill and Jeremy I had gone to Andrée to present it to her.

We'd surprised her, the three of us, and now I was saying goodbye, standing on her porch, already missing her. Then her husband pushed through the yammering screen door, thinner than I'd remembered him but looking calm and good. "Andrée," he said in his heavy, slurring accent, "I've been trying hard but it's no good. I don't know what's wrong. I can't fix it right now, but I promise: I'll fix it soon." His dark, thick bangs swung boyishly into his eyes, and he cocked his head to clear his vision. Openly, unabashedly, he flirted with his wife, winning her forgiveness for whatever failure had occurred. Her cheeks turning pink, her lips relenting in a smile, Andrée knocked him lightly on the shoulder with her fist. It was a private moment between two people whose marriage had been a tortured uphill climb. Noticing me then, Andrée's husband waved, then waved toward the car—a frenetic, stumpy wave—where Bill and Jeremy were waiting. "He's finally quit smoking," Andrée said after he was back inside, "and now he complains that his life is no good because he doesn't have a vice." She shook her head, and her smile was still coming as she looked with longing toward the shadows of their house. *They're friends*, I remember thinking. *They made it. They're friends.* And this is the strand of them that I'll keep alive, for when Andrée needs to find it, on this page.

18

River Wise

WE GO AS FAR AWAY as we can, to a town chosen from the pages of a catalog when winter was at its darkest and most claustrophobic. It takes us more than a day to complete our travels, finally descending a black thread of mountain road with nothing but gravity at the edge. A single distraction at the wheel, I think, and we'd start cracking into atoms. We'd fall and fall and fall, and only the sheep and the cows would lift their heads and notice.

In the end the road weaves itself into a valley. Out of danger, we're suddenly deep in the heart of St. Eulalie, on fire with lush geraniums. Red and candy pink, they flame up out of window boxes, urns, and fountains, out of strained wooden barrels and deconstructed wagon wheels, the baskets of old-fashioned bicycles. They sizzle like weeds among stalks of corn and orange pumpkins, among chickens and dogs, on the sodden roofs of abandoned houses.

There's only one way to go, and that's to squeeze the car between the massive half-timbered buildings, waiting for the old men in berets, supporting their weight on their canes, to step aside and let us through. They wave to us as if we belong, and we wave back, tentatively. American interlopers in the unadulterated southwest of France.

Our house looks just as it did in the catalog, only more essential, part of the bracelet of buildings that circumscribe the crushed-stone plaza. Behind it lies the river, wide and gray green. The whole scene is lit like a Maxfield Parrish canvas: doors, shutters, planters, the cantankerous fish in the river, throw off sparks of amber. I see a puff of white escape the baker's window, a clap of flour that takes to the skies.

There are no phones here; nobody speaks our language. We have left everything behind. We're on our own in St. Eulalie. Exhausted and hungry, we park our car, unload our things, and start meandering aimlessly. We're out of the town in ten minutes, suddenly emptied onto a long dirt road, among milky brown cows and newly naked sheep, more rows of corn, beside a quiet graveyard from which an old woman emerges, dead flowers in one fist, a silver bucket in the other. We circle back through the town, past the chugging water wheel, and climb the steps to our rental. While my husband operates the big-toothed key, I watch the five old men hunched together on a smooth-planked bench across the plaza. I watch them lean together conspiratorially, shake their heads, and cackle. I watch them listen to each other kindly as they wheel their broken leather shoes around the elegant hubs of their ankles.

They are there the next morning and the next afternoon, and they are there throughout our stay in the old stone house that was once a barn, which is the first to receive the resonant bells of the hour. Only in the heat of the afternoon do these five fast friends of St. Eulalie disappear, slipping back into their own houses, which I have learned to identify. If there are other people inside those houses, they never greet the open air. It's the men I see at night watering their red geraniums, in the morning at the bakery, waiting for their single loaf of bread. One man, with a bright white mole like a permanent tear below his eye, wears the same pale blue vest every day. The man whose bench they gather on wears a swirly nylon shirt of purple and gray. Sometimes a farmer lady from the edge of town bicycles in, and the men slide over on the bench. Sometimes a dog yaps its way into the talk. The men christen its head with their gentle hands, and never lose pace with the friendship.

Little by little, in St. Eulalie, we try out our French, relinquish bad habits. We learn when to wait in line for our croissants and when to shut our shutters, when the mosquitoes won't attack and when the cows will come to nudge us. Jeremy is the most facile of us three — walking the long river road for hours without complaining, sleeping unperturbed through the midnight bells, making friends at the café, where he settles down with Popsicles and a strange red drink and proves commendably fearless with his own brand of flattened French. We venture out to other villages, risking our lives on perilous gorge roads. But from the start our loyalty is to St. Eulalie, where the baker adds our daily order to his list and a table awaits us at the café. The old men on the bench nod cordial greetings. The man who whisks the plaza clean teaches Jeremy a game he calls *petanque*. Sturdy, foreshortened women dousing their geraniums at night put their palms on our shoulders, sweep their chins toward their houses, and tell us village gossip we only partly understand. *This house belonged to my mother and to her mother and to my mother's mother before that,* one says. *And isn't it pretty, look at the doorknob.* Another, indicating a slate-roofed shambles across the street, says river rocks last a thousand years: stand here, imagine how this old barn looked when it was new. Down the road even farther, a woman goes on about the merits of her cooking while a yard full of hens twitter suspiciously, and her poodle, ancient and satiated, lolls in the cradle of her arms.

At night the bells deliver the religion of the hour. We hear the fish in the river skimming moonlight. We contemplate the ruins near the cow path at the edge of the village, and what might happen if we stayed behind to fix it up. *Joanne,* I write, in the shadows before dawn. *If we didn't come home from St. Eulalie, would you write to me, and would you visit?* I make notes I will never reference about changelessness and five old men, friendships that have a lifetime to put down roots. About Patrick, one of the rare young men in town, who runs the café and has temporarily adopted my son and speaks with quiet, puffing, eternal *p*'s. *I will write about you,* I tell him one day, and he blushes, not knowing what I mean. I listen to the fish leap at night.

In the daylight, there are the five old men on the bench and whoever happens by, mostly the lady on the bicycle in the predictable red and orange dress, who dismounts, throws her hip out sideways, and returns strands of rusty hair to the unraveled chignon at her neck. From my balcony I spy on them, wait for the long pause in their conversation, but it never seems to come. I wonder what they have to say, what there is to report on, what might have changed since their last gathering on the bench. What is left to talk about among men who, Patrick says, have lived in St. Eulalie all their lives, in houses handed down to

them, in homes without wives? If it's the weather they're discussing, it hasn't changed, save for one splendid night of driving rain. If it's the river, it seems sublimely set in its ways, sedate, as it goes about its business of connecting town to town. And if it's memories, what haven't they already revived so many times that it's physical, as self-evident and reliable as the friends themselves seem to be?

Something fills in me and spills, and I am nostalgic for a time I never knew, for a place, a community, that values friendship above all. "Patrick," I ask at the café one afternoon, "are you friends with the old men on the bench?"

He puts his lips together and a sound escapes, his soft, elusive *p.* "Friends," he tells me in French, in the undertow of a sigh, "are the important ones, the ones who matter most, like family." He pulls the smoke through his cigarette, then lets it out to the sky.

"And the men?" I ask.

"I know them well," he says. "But I have friends of my own." There's something sweet about his certainty. This is the gift of a life moved forward by nothing save a river and church bells.

I write letters home about St. Eulalie; I never manage to mail them. I take photographs, but I know that every time the shutter clicks I have failed to distill the essence of the scene. It's longevity that matters here, the invisible webbings between people, the cascade of red geraniums from windows. What is accomplished in St. Eulalie is life itself, and that life shared with others, and what breaks my heart is the stories I'll never hear, the scaffolds I'll never see, the irrelevancy of the few spare things that can, in fact, be explained. I miss my own friends more as the days go by, seem to see them with greater clarity

here. I miss the things I know they've given me, things I've never thanked them for.

Maybe we have to go far from home to see all that friendship is. Maybe we have to sit in the sun with a river behind us to catch our breath at the unplanned interludes that make us who we've been. For some reason it's the image of Bambi breezing through my front door that strikes me now. Bambi buoyantly stopping by, unannounced, to sit on my couch and not mind the mess and talk about a big Wyoming sky. And now the sprawling family at the Radford house—always a baby on Mary's arm, a kid on Greg's square shoulders, a room to kick our shoes off and sink into comfortable conversation. I think about those whom I'm only just now getting to know, the stories they tell me, the passions they share, the small disclosures they entrust me with, a way of saying that I'm becoming part of them. And, of course, I think about Joanne, her voice, her notes, her common sense, the language we conceived and I buried and she's pulled up out of the earth again like a spray of flowers.

Some friendships begin with a slow, quiet drawl; others bang into being. There are moments, filters, tests that fortify some ties and snuff out others. Friends are the multicolored cloaks we wear, the circles we draw around us, the chores we share, the letters we wait for, the gifts we want to buy, the heartaches we take on as our own, the place we turn with our fears, our wants, our sadness. Friends are there even when they are not; we talk to them in our heads. *I wish you could see this. I wish you were here. I would like to know what you'd say if you were on this balcony, in this sun, watching the baker send his flour up as clouds.* Who knows what needle takes what thread and seams two people together. There is nothing less tangible than friendship and very little so potent.

What will we say to Patrick when we pack our things to go, knowing that we'll never see him again and that we won't forget him? Patrick, who is part of us now, the way the five men on the bench in the plaza are part of my understanding of friendship. How will we—Bill, Jeremy, and I—manage our goodbyes?

"What if we bought that ruin at the end of the street?" I ask Bill on our last night in the dark, in the echo of church bells.

"I don't know," he says, awake to the night sounds too. "Those ruins would make a beautiful home." Another set of bells sings out, and then the plaza is still. "Could you survive," he asks, "in a place like this, a place so quiet? Being so young in a town that's so old, and nobody speaking our language?"

"But we'd learn French," I say, not believing myself. "And we'd learn to appreciate the silence. And we'd make the house so big that we would never be alone. Our friends would come, and our families. We could bring the people we love here, to us."

"I don't know," Bill says, taking my hand. "I just don't know. But can you hear the river outside?"

"Yes," I say, because I hear it moving on, in search of all the villages beyond us.

19

Rendezvous

WE RENDEZVOUS at the old farmer's market on Saturday morning, half past ten. It's a circus inside, the way food and ethnicity make a circus—the Amish girls in their hairnets promoting cheese; the old Greek couple guarding their marinated olives; the Jewish man hawking his bread; the wealthy chocolatiers; the Mexicanas; the crowd weaving among them.

The serious buyers have come and gone—people expecting guests, those who placed their orders the week before, those who come at dawn for the mild adventure of flowers stuffed beside sausage stuffed beside the corrugated boxes of speckled quail's eggs. The ten-thirty crowd is leisurely and forgiving, social, glad for the bottlenecks between aisles, the conversations that tickle on about recipes and party favors, petits fours, duck sauce, the remaindered cantaloupes, easy hors d'oeuvres. Whoever grew up in these parts and stayed comes to the farmer's market on Saturday morning, and it is for the chance of encountering these people that Joanne, now an outsider here, has come. She lifts her eyes to the crowd and I know that she hasn't seen me yet.

She looks (and there is only one word for this) regal. If she has to exert herself against her mother's wheelchair, it doesn't show. The grand chair seems to float out on its own, its handles giving Joanne's palms a place to rest, Joanne's mother willing it forward. Joanne is wearing her kids like jewelry—Samantha dangling delicately on her left wrist, Michael, more boyish tough, on her right.

"Hey," I say when I'm close enough.

"Hey," she answers.

"Well?" I ask.

"Let's just walk around."

It's harder to get through the crowd with a wheelchair, so we take our time navigating the bulge that aprons out around the soft twisting pretzels, the organic yams, the little individual pans of chicken cordon bleu, none of which we are inclined to buy. Jeremy, who until this moment has been gliding silently by my side, decides to break loose, and with a little kick of his head, he's off toward the glass bakery case, where they sell cakes made to look like entrées—sculpted confections mimicking hot dogs and hoagies, watermelon slices with little black icing ants. Jeremy can never believe that these are cakes, and now Michael, also loose, is at his side, pressing his face against the glass so that his lips deposit a little frosted O.

"No way," Michael says, when Jeremy explains what's in the case.

"Yup," Jeremy answers. "Just cakes."

I lean down to ask Joanne's mother how she's doing, and she insists, as she has been lately, that I call her by her first name. "I don't know if I can do that," I tell her, and she says, "You better hurry up and learn," half joking, half asserting, the stroke having proved impotent against my old best friend's mother's wit. "I'll give it a try, Mrs. F.," I tell her, and she slaps her one good thigh with her one good hand and rolls her eyes in my direction.

"What are you looking to buy?" I ask Joanne, and she smiles, shrugs. "I'm just here for the entertainment," she says, and we walk comfortably together, no need to talk, our friendship big enough for this, grown up enough to take in companionability. Our boys are moving slightly ahead. Michael has a compass and some gum, both of which he shares with Jeremy. Samantha wants a cookie and she gets a frosted one.

Pedestrian traffic moves in both directions. Slowly. Connections are made all around, knots form and unravel as one person recognizes another, whole families intersect, kids go off arm in arm, fresh dollars in their hands. At the sausage counter, friends who have more than a few things to say arrange themselves on the splintery stools, tell the girl at the griddle how they'd like their eggs, and set up camp, big brown bags at their feet, elbows touching, their news splashing from ear to ear. Across a dozen other counters, proprietors and customers trade the week's information, the latest gossip, while behind the counters the Amish talk to Amish, Greek talks to Greek, teenagers talk to teenagers, the old man says something to the young kid about apples, everyone exchanging tales. Friendship of every hue and variety is on display—glancing, time-tested, discrepant friendships between teacher and pupil, buyer and seller, neighbor and neighbor, mother and daughter, recently reacquainted hearts. There is a good feeling here, a sense of community and kinship, the way every village ought to feel, even if it's the suburbs. Michael and Jeremy pull ahead in the crowd; overly motherly, I call them back.

"Just let them go," Joanne says. "What can happen? Look where we are."

The kids look from me to Joanne, back to me again, pleading and hopeful. "You're not leaving the building, okay?" I tell them, duly parental. "Promise me that. No going through doors." Both nod, two giant gallops with their heads, then quickly turn and head off before I can change my mind — Jeremy skipping, Michael pulling on Jeremy's arm, both of them weaving through the morass of strollers, talkers, buyers. I watch them go, standing on tiptoe as they pass from sight.

"They're fine," Joanne says to me, reading my mind as she always could.

I sigh, sounding the way I feel, which is unconvinced.

"You know," Joanne says, a smile tipping her lips. "You've got to start letting go. Jeremy's one hundred percent ready for this world. And this is just the farmer's market. On a Saturday."

"No one," I counter, "is ever ready for this world," but of course I know what she means, and I smile, if only to myself. It's the old Joanne who just told me that, the Joanne I always trusted to speak her mind, to be forthright, to counter my shyness, my nerves, to break me out of my confining point of view. "How are you doing down there, Mrs. F.?" I call. The good lady in the wheelchair slaps her one good thigh with her one good hand and audibly, humorously sighs.

Joanne gives me a look I remember, a look that says volumes about the way she really feels, though she laughs now for the sake of her mother. *My mother,* Joanne's eyes say, *doesn't belong in this damned wheelchair. My mother should be walking beside us.* With our old Morse code, I let Joanne know that I heard what she didn't say, that I too am horrified by what has happened, that I honor, detail by detail, the story Joanne has recently told me about the stroke that took this woman down in the heart of a cruise, in the middle of the ocean, just like that, no warning signs. I honor the emergency helicopter that took her mother ashore, the helicopter that carried her back to the States, the months and years of rehabilitation, the partial recovery despite the desertion by friends who saw that she would no longer be as quick at bridge, would need to be helped from place to place. I honor Joanne's father, who loves his wife now more than ever, who has flowers delivered every Friday to their door. *I know how you feel,* I say to Joanne without speaking, because my mother, too, and my family, has suffered injury, the arc of recovery, desertions of opportunities and dreams. So we have shared this, too, this loss of innocence with our mothers, and we share it now in the noise of the market, our two sons running up ahead. We will share it always, it's lodged within who we are.

"Who are you looking for?" I ask Joanne.

"I don't know." She smiles. "I suppose anyone I can remember."

"Beware of wrinkles," I say. "Everyone we used to know has aged by twenty years."

"God," Joanne says. She shakes her head. "God. Twenty years."

We've gone up one aisle and down another and are turning the corner on a third. Samantha has finished what she wants of the cookie; Joanne tosses the rest away. "I'm going to look for the boys," I tell Joanne, and her eyes tell me that I'm being overprotective but that she'll love me nonetheless, and with that blessing, such as it is, I circle the wheelchair and start slipping through the buzz.

I'll always risk anything to get a quick glimpse of my son. I go up and down the aisles in this biggish, well-lit place. At last I spot Michael and Jeremy at the long glass counter that houses the perennially popular Weaver's Cheese. They're offering each other cheeses from the sample tray, passing the squares of cheddar like wafers at communion. I pull up short before they see me, then watch as they toss their toothpicks on the cement floor and hover over Michael's new compass. Michael says something and Jeremy throws his head back and laughs, and then they trot off in the compass-suggested direction. I about-face and travel upstream in the crowd until I find Joanne, who has bought two loaves of raisin bread and is standing in line for grapes. Samantha has impatiently begun to twine around her arm.

"The boys are fine," I report after I've made my way to her.

"What did I tell you," Joanne says. "They're growing up."

"How you doing, Mrs. — " I lean down.

"Don't you start with me," she jokes, interrupting. "Don't start with me, Beth. Mrs. F.," she mutters. "Mrs. F."

"So guess who's standing over in the corner?" I say to Joanne, after I canvass the fruit stand. "It's old Carrie Murphy. Remember her?"

Just as she used to in high school, Joanne starts taking careful, pecking peeks until she's got Carrie Murphy in her view. I almost crack up with the moment, the memories, with the way Joanne does a parody of discretion while being the most obvious spy in the world. "Oh, my God," she says. "You're right. That's Carrie Murphy. Look at her. She's got at least four or five kids." We both stare without shame at the woman with the familiar haircut who's checking out apples across the way. "Oh, my God," Joanne says. "She must be close to forty. And if she is, what in the hell does that make us?"

"Probably middle-aged," comes the response from the

wheelchair, and I lean down, joking: "Didn't ask you, Mrs. F., but thanks just the same."

"I'm going to go talk to her," Joanne says, and I say, "Oh, please. No. Tell me you're not."

"Why not?" Joanne says, a smile darting across her lips. "What's to lose? Are you still a coward about these things?"

"I need to go check on the boys," I tell Joanne, and she rolls her eyes theatrically at me.

"You're still so hopeless, Beth. Hopeless. Hopeless. Hopeless."

"I know."

"I never did teach you to throw caution to the winds."

"Have fun with Carrie," I tell Joanne. "Tell her hello for me, okay?" I pat Samantha on the head and wink at Mrs. F., and once again I'm touring the market.

This time it takes a while to find Jeremy and Michael. Though I know they're safe, my heart starts to thump in my chest after I've passed every stall and still haven't discovered them. I consider going outside and checking the parking lot, but even I know that that would be crazy. They're somewhere inside. Up and down I walk again—past purple tulips, faded piñatas, fancy fruit tarts, big shanks of meat, blue fish. All of a sudden I hear Jeremy calling me from behind.

"We've found the perfect thing," he announces, using his emcee voice, when I turn. "Follow us. We'll point it out." Serious, competent, Michael checks his compass, consults with Jeremy. In sync, they spin on their heels and start marching away. Jeremy's sudden independence in this market is not lost on me, the flat-out fun he's having, the way he, because of the windfall companionship of a bright, brave kid his own age, is taking on all the chaos. Friendship will do that, freeing us to find more of ourselves. I walk in their shadow now—following them, weaving with them in and out of the crowds, in and out of the spell they're casting, in and out of themselves. The whole time they're gamboling, they're whispering, laughing to each other, checking the compass, firm on their feet. I walk behind, a little awestruck. Finally they come to the tiny poultry man, whose ducks and geese look simply naked instead of dead.

"Let's take one of these home." Jeremy turns and addresses me. For a reason known only to the boys—their secret—this is the prize at the end of their hunt, and it's a glory.

"As a pet?" I tease. "You want to take this goose home as a pet?"

Jeremy goes hysterically silly. "No," he says, busting up. "Not as a pet. For dinner, Mom. For dinner. Let's take him home." Michael nods in agreement, mission accomplished. I can't imagine the game they'd set themselves to play, but for now we have our denouement.

Shaking my head, I smile a negative at the poultry man in his pink-stained apron, who is ready to carve if I do the bidding. "Maybe next week," I tell him, pretty sure that I'll return and look for him and that he'll remember me. "In the meantime, thanks for giving these little shoppers here a thrill." Jeremy feigns disappointment over the unconsummated purchase. Michael peers down at his compass. I tell the kids that if they come with me, I'll buy them candy, a sentiment that soon wins the day.

All three together, we make our way to the sophisticated chocolatiers, whose fancy glass case sits directly across from the fruit, where, sure enough, Joanne is cavorting with a pleasantly surprised Carrie, saying some things I can guess, some things I cannot, while Samantha slithers up her mother's arm and Mrs. F. waits peacefully, resolutely in her wheelchair. Around Joanne there is confusion and sweet chaos, as friendships tangle and food changes hands and voices call out: *See you next week, Jim. Good to see you, Mindy. Mom, can't I go over to Toby's to play?* Beside me, savoring their chocolates, checking the compass, are Michael and Jeremy, ripe with adventure, destined, over their lifetimes, for the exhilaration, the disappointments, the confusion, the triumphs, the risks, the responsibilities, and the succoring that friendship will bring.

Joanne, I think, as I stand alone in the milling crowd, you are the friend I lost and found, the friend I'm still finding out. And when we are old and our friendship has again made itself into something new and is again preserved as something old, I will remember this day and the lace of your hair, and the way your feet plant themselves, a little crooked, on this floor.

Acknowledgments

This is a book of memory and a quest, a story I could not have told without the many friends who have entered my life and, like artists, have helped shape it. To those who have allowed me to tell our stories here, I am, and always will be, grateful for their friendship and their abundant generosity. To Julie and her family of exquisite developmentally challenged adults, whose names and identities I have elected to alter, I extend deep gratitude across these pages. To my parents, brother, and sister, I am grateful as well, for their integrity, gracious good sense, and family fellowship.

To Linda, River, and June at the Leeway Foundation I am indebted, not just for their beneficent funding, but for the grace of their faith in a book that, early on, I barely understood myself. To the National Endowment for the Arts, whose grant provided hope, courage, and time, I extend a most profound gratitude. To Sylvie Rabineau, I want to say thank you, for believing and for saying so. To Ellen Ryder, a question: where would I be without your reliable intelligence and wit? I am deeply thankful to Amy

Rennert, my literary agent, for all that she has done on behalf of my writing, and for all that she has done and said and imagined on behalf of our friendship. And finally, to Anton Mueller, my editor; Peg Anderson, manuscript editor extraordinaire; Betsy Peterson, legal counsel and kind heart; and the entire team at Houghton Mifflin, I offer everlasting thanks, for the conversations and care that enriched this book and made its writing matter.